THE CARDMAKER'S
workbook

DISCARD

THE CARDMAKER'S
workbook

The Complete Guide to **Design, Color, and Construction Techniques** for Beautiful Cards

Jenn Mason

BEVERLY MASSACHUSETTS

QUARRY BOOKS

First published in the United States of America by
Quarry Books, a member of
Quayside Publishing Group
100 Cummings Center
Suite 406-L
Beverly, Massachusetts 01915-6101
Telephone: (978) 282-9590
Fax: (978) 283-2742
www.quarrybooks.com

Library of Congress Cataloging-in-Publication Data

Mason, Jenn.
   The card makers workbook / by Jenn Mason.
      p. cm.
   ISBN 1-59253-415-5
   1. Greeting cards. 2. Handicraft. I. Title.
   TT872.M3175 2008
   745.594'1--dc22

                        2007039180

ISBN-13: 978-1-59253-415-9

ISBN-10: 1-59253-415-5

10 9 8 7 6 5 4 3 2 1

Cover Design: Silke Braun
Cover Image: Al Mallette, Lightstream
Design: Rachel Fitzgibbon
Illustrations: Jenn Mason
Templates: Jenn Mason

Printed in Singapore

"I like opening a letter and thinking myself loved."

—Virginia Woolf

Contents

i love you.

Introduction

The design principles used to create great cards are not exclusive to these small works of creativity—they are relevant to all types of art. Collage artists, painters, interior designers, cake decorators, and graphic designers all use composition, balance, color, construction, and a variety of techniques in their work. And they are all interested in new tools to help them design. Good design is achieved by translating or reinterpreting an idea, concept, or visual trigger in a unique and graphically pleasing way. When I teach a workshop, I tell my students that it's not as important to take away the project we're making as it is to be inspired by the creative process and the design principles they're learning, so they can take this knowledge home and use it to make something new and different.

This workbook is divided into chapters that will walk you through the process of seeing composition, colors, and supplies in new ways. My goal, as I made card after card (after card), was to create a book that inspired each reader in a different way. If you are new to cardmaking, this book can help you discover a new world of creativity. If you're an old pro, this book can help you explore new ways of looking at colors, construction, and supplies and re-energize your creativity when you find yourself in a rut.

Chapter 1 discusses composition and card design. We'll see examples of balance and well-placed focal points. We'll look at repetition as a design element, as well as scale and texture. Color and all its related theory is summed up for you in Chapter 2, with easy to understand terminology that will help you choose color combinations that work. Chapter 3 is all about construction and what you can create when you think beyond a simple, rectangular, folded card. Chapter 4 is for the penny pincher in all of us and offers ideas on how to stretch your supplies by using them in different ways for varied outcomes.

I haven't forgotten those long hours of working on holiday cards. In Chapter 5, I focus on methods, such as simplifying and buying smart, for making multiple cards more efficiently, and I'll also show you how to make the perfect wrap or portfolio for presenting a set of cards as a gift. Finally, Chapter 6 covers the ins and outs of card making, with instructions for creating envelopes from scratch and lining them. It also includes an extensive list of sentiments for your cards.

This book is not just about the basics of design, it is a tool to point you in the direction of untold creativity. Use it as your diving board, then get on your swimsuit and bathing cap and dive in!

—*Jenn Mason*

Tools & Techniques

You don't need much to make a card. You can create one with nothing more than a piece of paper, a stamp or embellishment, and a little time. This isn't to say that you couldn't take advantage of the wide range of supplies available at paper and craft stores—quite the contrary. In very little time, and with a lot of money, you can easily amass (or should I say "collect"?) numerous card making tools, accessories, and embellishments, from very affordable eyelets (see page 124) and brads at a couple of cents apiece to the extravagant-but-once-you-have-it-you-won't-know-how-to-live-without-it electronic die cutting machine (see page 126).

I can't possibly describe all the items you might possibly use in card making, but I can cover some basics and give you a brief primer on a few techniques—setting those eyelets, for example, and using rubber stamps.

First, the Supplies

Every good card maker has paper and something to cut, glue, and decorate it with. So, that's where we'll start.

PAPER IT

The number one rule here is, "You get what you pay for." Inferior paper makes inferior cards. Two basic types of paper are used in card making: cardstock and decorative paper, which you can find in solid colors or printed with a design. What should you buy? Whatever makes your heart sing! If you haven't traveled down the scrapbook aisles at the craft store lately, treat yourself to a trip. The number of papers available has exploded. And here's a tip: Scrapbook manufacturers introduce new paper lines as often as every six months, so you'll always find new designs to feed your paper addiction.

CUT IT

Unless you've purchased a pack of blank cards, you will need to cut your paper. I suggest buying a paper trimmer with a small, replaceable cutting blade that slides back and forth to cut the paper. A number of companies make these; if you're not sure which one to choose, talk to creative friends and ask them for recommendations. (And don't forget to buy extra blades!) If you don't want to use a paper trimmer, you can always resort to the old standbys: the metal edge ruler, cutting mat, and craft blade.

I also keep a nice, sharp pair of small detail scissors on my work table. These are not expensive, so don't get them from the dollar store; they will dull too quickly. A good pair of scissors can slice through ribbon "like buttah."

Another great cutting tool, when used correctly, is a pair of decorative edge scissors. There are many different blades, but you will be well served with pinking shears, scalloped, and deckle edge styles.

GLUE IT

For adhering bulky items onto a card, quick-dry tacky glue is my best friend. The acid-free glue stick, another of my adhesives of choice, is especially useful for adhering small and oddly shaped items. When I want to work quickly, I use an adhesive runner that lays down a film of adhesive in no time. And, finally, if I want to add dimension, I adhere elements with adhesive foam tape, dots, or squares.

DECORATE IT

The list of items that you can add to cards is endless, but here is a good start: stickers, rub-ons, brads, eyelets, staples, ribbons, waxed twine, tags, wire, binder clips, glitter, gel pens, decorative paper clips, and chipboard embellishments.

CREATE IT

This section wouldn't be complete without a list of the tools needed to create the endless variations of cards in this book. Keep in mind that collecting supplies and tools is addictive! The tools I like to use include an awl, stamps and inks, embossing powders and a heat gun, paper punches, die cut tools, sponge daubers, corner rounders, a Design Runner (a portable personal printer made by Xyron), eyelet setters (eyelets are useless without them!), hole punches (¼", ⅛", and ¹⁄₁₆" will do, a bone folder (for making great folds), black Micron pens, and a good ruler.

Second, the Techniques

FOLDING PAPER

Paper folds better in one direction than the other. To test this, lightly hold your chosen piece of paper in front of you, with one hand on each side.

Bring your hands toward each other, letting the paper bend in the middle, and note the resistance.

Rotate the paper 90 degrees, and repeat the test, again noting the paper's resistance to bending.

Now, hold the paper in front of you in the direction that provides the least resistance—you'll find that the grain of the paper is vertical. (To remember this, you can draw a light arrow in pencil on the paper.)

When you cut the paper, you want the fold to be parallel to the grain of the paper. If you've ever folded a card and created a fold that was jagged or uneven, it was because you folded against the grain. If you must fold against the grain, score the paper first. You can use the scoring tool that comes with the paper trimmer, or you can create a score by simply tracing the fold line using the edge of a bone folder and a ruler. Either way, once you've folded your paper, go back over the fold with the bone folder to get a really crisp fold.

STAMPING

Although this book is not about stamping, a lot of great stamps were inked in the making of it. If you really want to get into stamping, I recommend finding a local stamp store and checking out the class schedule—you'll be amazed at what you can create with stamps.

To ink a stamp, tamp the stamp once or twice on an ink pad to cover the image with ink.

Check the stamp before stamping it on paper, to ensure that the entire surface is covered with ink.

Then, with even pressure, stamp the image onto your paper—without rocking the stamp back and forth—and pull up.

EMBOSSING

If you want to emboss a stamped image, you will need to use pigment ink or embossing ink. These inks stay wet longer, so that you can sprinkle embossing powder over them.

1. Stamp the image.

2. Sprinkle embossing powder over the image and tap off the excess powder, so that only the powder covered image shows.

3. Use a heat gun to slowly heat the powder until it melts.

SETTING AN EYELET

You'll find a number of eyelet setting tools on the market these days. Some clamp down on the eyelet like pliers, some need to be hit with a tool and a hammer. It is best to follow the instructions that come with your particular tool, but the basics are as follows.

1. Punch a hole where you want to place the eyelet.

2. Drop the eyelet into the hole and, with your finger over the eyelet, flip the paper over. Carefully slide out your finger.

3. Place the eyelet setting tool into the eyelet and hit it with the hammer until the eyelet locks into the paper.

USING A GLUE STICK

Some people avoid using glue sticks to adhere papers together because they find that the glue doesn't hold. You can solve this problem by ensuring that you give your papers sufficient coverage. To get glue all the way to the edges of the paper, run the glue stick off the edges onto the page of an old phone book. Once you have glued your paper, flip to the next page for a clean surface!

To get good adhesion, after gluing your papers together, burnish them with your hands or with the bone folder while the glue is still wet.

Downloading the Templates

Throughout the following chapters, you'll find projects that call for templates. You can find these templates, listed by project, online at the address listed below.

Use the following directions to download and print the templates you need.

Materials

- Computer
- Scanning program (such as Photoshop)
- Printer
- Paper (see project instructions for appropriate type)

to download...

1. Log on to www.quarrybooks.com/cardmaker and find the appropriate template.

2. Open your scanning program and then open the assigned template within the program.

3. Load your printer with some plain white paper. This will be your test paper. Print the template onto the paper and see how it looks. If the image appears too dark or too light, open the Image > Adjustments> Brightness/Contrast menu. Move the arrow up or down to get an image that looks better to your eye.

4. Load the paper tray with the pape needed for the project you wish to make. This may vary according to your specific scanning program, so you may have to follow the software manual to get the effect you want.

5. Print out the template and follow the project's directions for trimming and folding.

Composition

We all use composition in some way in our every day lives: when we decorate a cake, arrange books on a bookshelf, choose an outfit, place our furniture, even when we serve up dinner.

Much of the time, using composition is inherent—we don't think about it, we just do it. If one candlestick on the mantel seems off balance, we add a second one on the opposite side, to create symmetry. We might anchor the candlestick with a small vase, to give weight to the arrangement, or add more candlesticks, to provide repetition. We use the same principles to design a card.

In this chapter, we'll look at balance and how it can be affected by placement, size, and color. We'll follow that with a discussion on focal points—how to make sure your cards have one, and how to know when they don't need one! Then, we'll look at repetition as a design principle and how it can be achieved through shape, rhythm, and size. Speaking of size, we'll also play with scale, a fun design element that can get you out of a creative rut. We'll finish the chapter with a study of texture and how you can use ribbon, embellishments, and even your choice of paper to add it to your card designs.

Although design is subjective, and there are really no rights or wrongs, when it comes to composition, there are "okays" and "greats."

Knowing how to use these techniques will not only help you understand how to fix an "okay" card, it will also help you create a "wow" card, right from the start.

Following the sections on balance, focal point, repetition, scale, and texture is a series of designer card sketches. Each sketch is accompanied by a variety of card designs, with differing degrees of completion time.

The next time you sit down to make a card, challenge yourself to work from one of the designer sketches in this chapter and see what kind of masterpiece you can create. I also suggest keeping a small sketch pad near your workspace, so that you can try sketching your own designs.

Balance

Using balance is like sitting on the teeter totter at the school playground. When no one sits on the other end, it's no fun. Add a friend to the other seat, however, and now you can do things like make her go up fast or slow or balance in the middle. How you use balance on a card can make the card either successful or "no fun."

In card design, balance can be achieved through symmetrical or asymmetrical layouts. Placement of a singular element, and contrasting dark and light colors or small and large elements, can affect the balance on a card design.

UNBALANCED COMPOSITION

The card on the left struggles with an unbalanced composition. The yellow mat is too close to the bottom of the card, a problem repeated by the white and yellow mats. The heart and the circle tag are not balancing each other and instead are making an awkward center spot on the card.

BALANCED COMPOSITION

The card on the right uses the same elements as the unbalanced card but cures the awkwardness with better placement. The yellow, brown, and white mats are placed to leave slightly more area at the bottom than the top. The heart is slightly larger, to compete with the ribbon, and is placed to the right. The round tag completes a vertical axis from the heart through the center of the ribbon.

SYMMETRICAL COMPOSITION

To create a symmetrical composition, divide a card down its vertical or horizontal center with chosen design elements. A vertical composition is created on this card by using two different backgrounds that meet in the center. Centering the multiple mats and the main focal point (the dress) creates a straightforward graphic design.

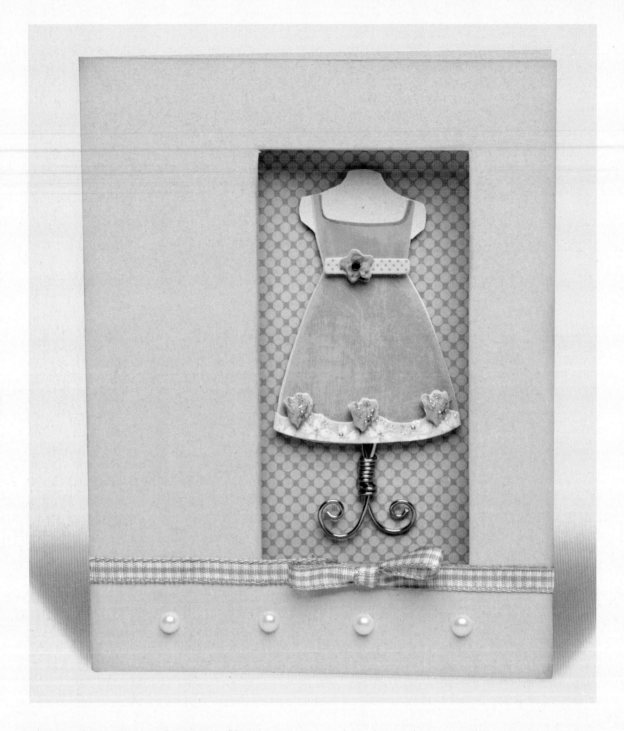

ASYMMETRICAL COMPOSITION

A pleasing asymmetrical layout is created by carefully placing elements to either the left or right of center or above or below the center of the card. On this card, the dress is seen through an off-center, rectangular cutout. The bottom trim, made of ribbon and pearl stickers, helps to balance the dress form and add to the card's overall style.

TOP 15 PEOPLE TO SEND CARDS TO

1. Your parents
2. Your children
3. Your wealthy spinster aunt and her seven cats
4. Your best friend
5. Your nieces and nephews in college (with homemade cookies)
6. Your future in laws
7. Your grandparents
8. Your grandchildren
9. Your paper boy
10. Your baby sitter
11. Your neighbor's gorgeous pool boy
12. Your favorite barista
13. Your priest, rabbi or spiritual mentor
14. Ben & Jerry's

"Sir, more than kisses, letters mingle souls."

—John Donne

Focal Point

The focal point is the star of the show. In many cases, this is the biggest or brightest element, but it can also be the most interesting, or "eye catching," area of the card. Although there are times when a card doesn't need a focal point, more often than not, a card is just begging for one. If you are creating a simple, patterned card that the recipient opens for a special message, your choice might be a simple, all-over pattern without a focal point. This works especially well for sets of blank note cards (see page 23).

Often a card lacks a focal point because all of the elements are given the same importance—what I call "wrapping paper syndrome." The colors may be beautiful, the individual items interesting, and the craftsmanship flawless, but the design could be repeated over and over again in a wrapping paper layout with no one special item calling attention to itself (see example on page 22). By adjusting the color, proportion, placement, or shape of the elements, you can fashion a successful focal point.

FOCAL POINT THROUGH COLOR

The card on the left uses the intense color of the magenta flower against the subtle, off-white of the tea cup to grab the viewer's attention. To be successful with a color focal point, you need to use a bit of that same color somewhere else on the card. Here, the magenta is found in the banding of the center strip.

FOCAL POINT THROUGH SCALE

The card on the right achieves a striking focal point by playing with scale. Here, the letter "B" on the tag is a large-scale representation of the lettering from the text placed underneath it. Manipulating the scale of letters, shapes, and embellishments can be a playful way to create a focal point.

FOCAL POINT THROUGH SHAPE

The focal point of the card on the left was created by combining three similar images with one of a different shape. The negative space around the bottom right heart is a clue to the eye to direct its attention there.

FOCAL POINT THROUGH PLACEMENT

For the card on the right, the embellishments were placed to create a focal point and lead the viewer's eyes to the message. The long border of fleur-de-lis on the right side of the card serves as an attention-grabbing background for the primary point of interest.

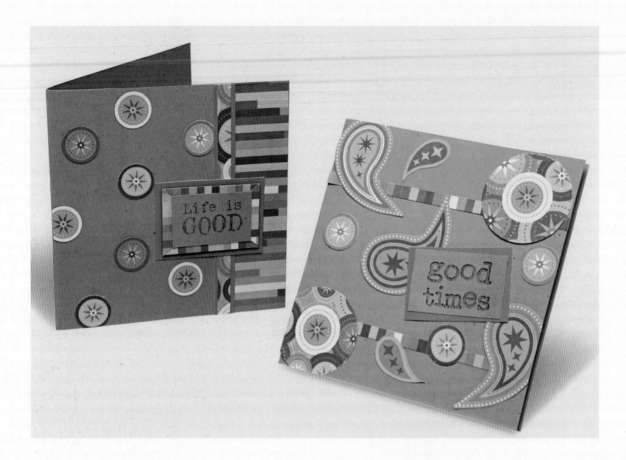

WRAPPING PAPER SYNDROME DEFINED

The culprit on the right is guilty of wrapping paper syndrome. Although composed of interesting and appealing colors, the card lacks a focal point. The patterned papers used for this card came in a coordinated pad. A paper pad can sometimes be a stumbling block for a card maker who wants to use all the papers at once.

WRAPPING PAPER SYNDROME CURED

Although the same elements were used on the card on the left, the result is a more cohesive look with a focal point in sight! By creating pattern with the dots and a side border with the paper, a perfect location for the card's message was formed, just slightly off to the bottom right of the card.

NO FOCAL POINT NEEDED

Not every card needs a focal point. There are times when an all-over patterned card will do the trick. This is especially true when creating blank note cards.

The example on the right is a true all-over patterned card, whose repeating pattern is broken by a simple aqua line showing from the card below. Although it has no focal point, the card on the left is accented by a little tag along the spine.

Repetition

Lather, rinse, repeat. It works for cards just like it works for shampoo. Well, maybe it should be "cut, glue, repeat." Using repetition is a great way to spice up a card layout. Using repeating elements, such as shape, color, and materials can turn a card from blah to wow! Repetition can also be used to create cohesiveness between the inside and outside of a card and the envelope.

REPETITION OF COLOR

The brilliant celery green color is repeated over and over on this card, in the sticker trim, flower brad, acetate letter "a," ribbon, and even the eyelet on the tag.

REPETITION OF SHAPE

Circles on the paper, circles in the background, and circles carrying the simple message on the front of this card (left) guide the viewer's eyes pleasingly around the card.

REPETITION OF MATERIALS

For this card, large and extra large brads were whimsically combined to create paw prints. The embossed metal photo corners and bone-shaped paper clip repeat the metallic glimmer throughout the card.

Scale

Playing with scale is one of my favorite creative "tools," and I use it all the time when I paint and create assemblages. I often ask myself what something will look like blown up to a large or even gigantic size. If I make it large enough, I can make the image abstract in appearance, something that is especially fun to do with images that are usually small and detailed. On the flip side, I like to play with commonly large items and rethink them in miniature. Playing with these juxtapositions is especially great for breaking through a creative block. Challenge yourself to enter the world of the giants or Lilliputians and discover what things look like when you change your perspective.

Use of scale also works well when you combine elements of different proportions on the same card. You can also use scale with other principles, such as repetition or focal point, to create beautiful designs.

LARGE AND SMALL SCALE COMBINED

The combination of large and small tea cups gives a lovely rhythm to the card on the left and creates a backdrop for a dramatic card wrap and sentiment.

LARGE SCALE

Although this tea cup might initially seem too large, once placed with an appropriate sentiment and set off with a dark mat, it becomes the perfect element for this card on the right.

SMALL SCALE

The diminutive size of the tea cups on the left-hand card is balanced by placing them in a group, which gives them heft and presence as the main focal point of the card.

NORMAL SCALE

With large and small sizes to play with, it's easy to forget the basic—normal scale. There is nothing boring about a well-designed card that uses elements in a normal scale, as is shown here in this elegantly simple card on the right.

Texture

Texture can be the crowning glory of any beautiful card. With the simple addition of a mat, ribbon, or textured piece of paper, a card design can go from acceptable to astounding. The examples that follow show a number of cards with and without texture. See how each design uses a small embellishment here or a paper choice there to completely change the feel of the card. The element of texture can work a lot like jewelry, adding sparkle, contrast, and interest simply by appealing to our sense of touch.

A background of transparent stamped and embossed flower images on the front of this card mimics the identical image peeking out from the inside. More texture, in the form of glass glitter for the flower center and shutters covered in text, further enhances the card.

Extravagant layers of manipulated paper showcase the use of texture in this card. A tag tied with a bow through its glossy grommet is matted onto one layer, which is matted on a second, pinking-sheared layer, and then mounted onto a decadent paper ruffle layer.

In another example of multiple textures, this card employs crocodile patterned paper, vintage brads with a lovely patina, and ripped paper with a small print. A subtle addition of clear glaze painted over the sentiment gives it a three-dimensional appearance.

15 WAYS TO GIVE A CARD

1. Snail mail
2. Attached to a present
3. Attached to diamond earrings
4. With flowers
5. With beer
6. On a pillow
7. In a briefcase
8. In a suitcase
9. Taped to mirror
10. Under the windshield wiper
11. In a lunch box
12. On a laptop
13. Pony express
14. Bike messenger
15. In person

"What a wonderful thing is the mail, capable of conveying across continents a warm human hand-clasp."

—Anonymous

Designer Sketch No. 1

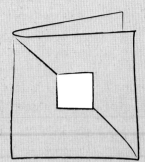

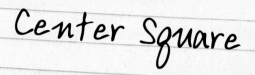

Example 1

1. Adhere a triangular piece of citrus green paper to the front of the card, and embellish it with a faux stitch rub-on.

2. Stamp a message onto a square of green decorative paper and emboss it in red.

3. Edge the piece with glitter and layer, using foam tape, onto a mat cut with mini-pinking shears.

4. Adhere this piece onto a larger piece of matching decorative paper.

5. Cut a square window from the front of the card, to reveal the message.

6. Use glue to make small dots on the front of the card and cover them with more glitter.

Example 2

1. Glue a square piece of decorative paper to the inside front of the card. Fold down the top right corner of the card to reveal the decorative paper.

2. Use a paper awl to poke holes, then secure the fold with waxed linen thread, using a blanket stitch.

3. Stamp the message onto a small square and attach it to the card with a binder embellishment.

4. To make the message pop, adhere a square of paper in a complementary color to the inside back of the card.

Example 3

1. Adhere a triangular piece of paper stamped with Versamark ink onto the card.

2. Add a series of small rectangles and a ribbon.

3. Decorate the top center rectangle with monogram rub-ons.

Designer Sketch No. 2

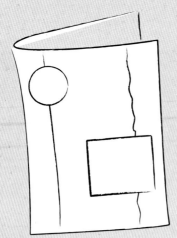

Example 1

1. Adhere a large piece of decorative paper onto the card to cover all but the left edge.

2. Add a strip of torn paper doodled with a black pen down the right side.

3. Attach a small paper flower to the card with a large, decorative brad.

4. Create a message of love by assembling four letter stickers on a piece of decorative paper and matting it onto a piece of cardstock cut with mini-pinking shears.

5. Adhere the message to the card with foam tape, to give dimension.

Example 2

1. Cover most of the card with decorative paper, leaving a spine exposed down the left side.
2. Place a sticker in the upper left corner.
3. With an awl, poke multiple holes through the card down the right side, then lace them with waxed twine.
4. For the main focal point, mat a photo and adhere it to the twine with foam tape.

Example 3

1. Adhere a strip of striped paper to the card, to give the illusion of a spine.
2. Punch a circle in the upper left corner, to create a window in the card.
3. Place a sticker inside the card, so that it shows through the window.
4. Mount a strip of ribbon layered with a sticker down the right side of the card, then layer it with another coordinating sticker.

Designer Sketch No. 3

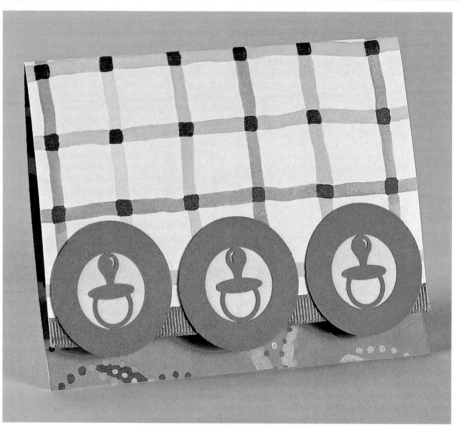

Example 1

1. Score and fold a piece of two-sided cardstock, so that the back is longer than the front and shows the inside pattern.

2. Glue grosgrain ribbon to the bottom edge of the card front.

3. To create the pacifier embellishments, punch a pacifier shape from a piece of blue paper.

4. Center a large circle punch, upside down, over the pacifier shape and punch it out. Repeat three times.

5. Back the pieces with yellow cardstock and adhere them to the lower edge of the card, over the ribbon.

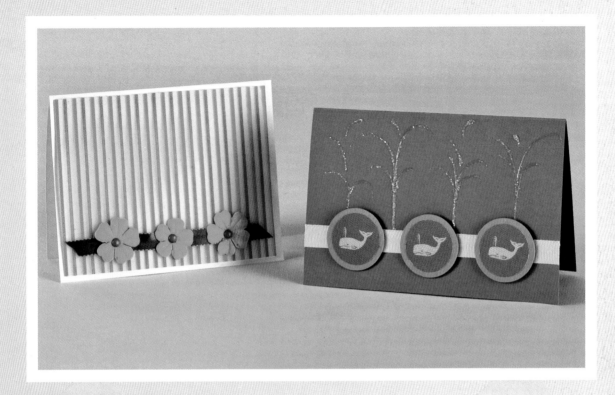

Example 2

1. Cut striped material from an inexpensive placemat and adhere it to the card with quick-dry tacky glue, being careful to apply the glue around the edge of the mat.

2. Cut a piece of ribbon on the diagonal and glue it to the striped mat.

3. Poke three holes in the ribbon with an awl, and attach three paper flowers to it with brads.

Example 3

1. Use quick-dry tacky glue to draw spouts of water onto the top two-thirds of the paper.

2. Pour glitter over the wet glue and tap the paper, to remove the excess glitter.

3. Add a strip of ribbon along the bottom of the spouts.

4. Use an upside-down circle punch to punch a whale from decorative paper. Repeat three times.

5. Center each whale circle onto a slightly larger punched circle.

6. Adhere the matted whale circles to the ribbon with foam tape.

Designer Sketch No. 4

Cinched

Example 1

1. Adhere decorative paper to a black card.

2. Add a sticker strip and coordinating winged heart sticker just below the center of the card. (Cut the sticker strip so that it doesn't show under the heart.)

3. Use alphabet stickers to write the word "LOVE" across the bottom of the card.

Example 2

1. Adhere decorative map paper to a cream card.

2. Punch a sunburst shape from teal cardstock and cut it with a craft knife, to create a paper buckle.

3. Layer pink decorative paper and blue cardstock to create a belt.

4. Thread the belt through the buckle and adhere to the card.

5. Stamp the word "Father" onto the card, and then enhance it with a Micron pen.

6. Sponge the card spine with green ink, to distress it.

Example 3

1. Tear a piece of pink decorative paper and adhere it to a kraft-colored card.

2. Place a strip of sheet music across the card.

3. Embellish the card with a butterfly sticker.

4. Add a rub-on sentiment to the bottom of the card.

Designer Sketch No. 5

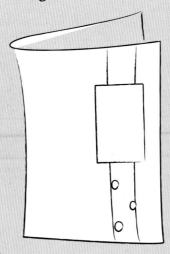

Dotted Stripe

Example 1

1. Cut a strip of decorative paper and adhere it to the right side of the card.

2. Stamp a sentiment onto a coordinating piece of decorative paper, cut it out, and adhere it to the strip with foam tape.

3. Tie a bow, trim the ends, and glue it to the sentiment with quick-dry tacky glue.

4. Use an awl to poke holes for the decorative brads and attach them.

Example 2

1. Cut three thin strips of cardstock and glue them to the right side of the card.

2. Use a rub-on to create a sentiment on a piece of cardstock.

3. Trim the sentiment and mat with another piece of cardstock.

4. Adhere the matted sentiment to the card with foam tape.

5. Use an awl to poke holes for the decorative pearl brads and attach them.

Example 3

1. Punch several shaped strips from two coordinating colors of cardstock and adhere them to a green card.

2. Add leather flower stickers to the strips, to create a bouquet.

3. Use an awl to poke holes for the large white brads along the strip and for the small, colored brads in the flower bouquet.

4. Attach the brads.

Designer Sketch No. 6

Example 1

1. Use glittered alphabet stickers to create a sentiment on a red card.

2. Using an awl, poke a hole in the bottom right corner and add the paper flower and leaves.

3. Add glass glitter to the brad in the flower with quick-dry tacky glue.

4. Use a hole punch and eyelet setter to add two eyelets to the upper right hand corner.

5. Tie two pieces of ribbon through the eyelets and trim.

Example 2

1. Tear a strip of green decorative paper and adhere it to a cream card.

2. Stamp the sentiment onto a piece of decorative paper and attach it to the card with a decorative binder clip.

3. Cut a circle from the bottom right corner to allow light to shine through the card front.

4. Attach a purchased label holder with image over the cutout with four brads. (Use an awl to poke the holes, if necessary.)

Example 3

1. Apply decorative rub-ons to a brick red card.

2. Create a label holder (downloadable template, Composition Card #1) from cardstock and add a label, using rub-ons.

3. Attach label holder to the card with three brads.

4. Stamp the chicken onto cream cardstock, and ink around the outer edge of the cardstock.

5. Add a final rub-on to the corner of the chicken piece and adhere it to the card.

Designer Sketch No. 7

Example 1

1. Use a Design Runner portable printer to print the message along the bottom of a teal card.

2. Cut a piece of white cardstock, then ink and manipulate the edges to give it a worn look.

3. Mount the white card to the teal card and add a layer of decorative teal paper.

4. Mount the four epoxy stickers onto white cardstock mats and adhere them to the card. (The "6" was added in a deliberately crooked fashion with foam tape.)

5. Add two coordinating small brads.

Example 2

1. Stamp the sentiment onto a piece of off-white cardstock and color it in with markers and Glaze gel pens (see Resources, page 156).

2. Layer the sentiment with decorative paper and another, larger piece of off-white cardstock and adhere it to the card.

3. Add three, three-dimensional purse stickers to the bottom of the card.

Example 3

1. Cut a square piece of gray cardstock, using wave or scallop edge scissors to cut two strips from the bottom of the card.

2. Adhere the pieces to a blue card.

3. Add three extra-large, decorative brads over the waves, using an awl to poke the holes.

4. Use a matte Glaze gel pen to write "surf's up" along the bottom of the card. (You can write it lightly in pencil first.)

Designer Sketch No. 8

Gatefold Glory

Example 1

1. Cut a piece of cardstock to make a card, but do not fold it.

2. Cut a piece of decorative paper the same width as the card but slightly shorter, and adhere it to the back of the cardstock.

3. Fold the card so that the ends meet in the middle, creating a gatefold card. The decorative paper should now show on the front of the card.

4. Cut a long strip of coordinating decorative paper and fold it into thirds, to create a decorative belt for the card.

5. Use an awl to poke holes in the ends, and secure a buckle onto the belt.

6. Tie small charms and flowers onto the buckle for decoration.

Example 2

1. Fold a piece of decorative cardstock into a gatefold card (see previous page).

2. Cut a rectangle of off-white paper slightly larger than the epoxy sticker sentiment and adhere it to the upper left corner.

3. Cut a piece of vellum long enough to wrap around the card but slightly shorter. Wrap it around the card.

4. Add the epoxy sticker sentiment onto the vellum over the off-white rectangle.

5. Create charms by filling a small brass frame with paper and a vintage stamp and by adhering small epoxy stickers to cardstock and cutting them out.

6. Add eyelets to the epoxy sticker charms.

7. Tie a piece of suede ribbon around the card, and attach the three charms to the ribbon with copper jump rings.

Example 3

1. Cut a piece of decorative paper slightly shorter and narrower than the card and adhere it to the back of the card.

2. Fold the card to create a gatefold (see previous page).

3. Use an awl to poke two holes for the decorative brads.

4. Tie a length of waxed twine to one of the brads and then attach both brads to the card.

5. Cut a tag from cardstock, crumple it, and distress it by rubbing ink over it.

6. Add a message and an eyelet to the distressed tag.

7. Use the waxed twine to tie the card closed, making sure to add the tag and key as decoration.

Designer Sketch No. 9

Banded Icon

Example 1

1. Lightly ink around the edge of a white card.

2. Tamp a stamp onto the ink pad, then spritz the stamp with water and stamp onto the card. Repeat as needed.

3. Overstamp the image once in the bottom right-hand corner, using a rainbow ink pad.

4. Outline the main image with quick-dry tacky glue and add glitter.

5. Use rub-ons and ink to create a label for the label holder and adhere both to the card, over the main image.

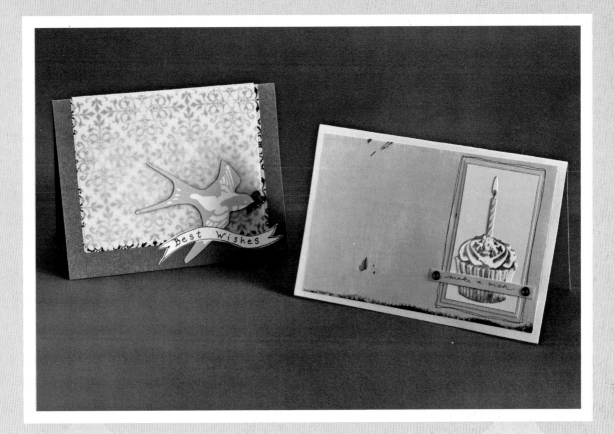

Example 2

1. Cut a piece of decorative paper and a slightly smaller piece of vellum and adhere both to the card.

2. Cut a small heart out of decorative paper and cover with glitter.

3. Add the heart to the beak of a bird sticker and adhere the sticker to the lower right corner of the card.

4. Cut a small banner (downloadable template, Composition, Card #2) from coordinating paper and write your message on the banner. (Practice with a pencil first.)

Example 3

1. Cut a piece of decorative paper slightly smaller than the card and attach it to the front.

2. Layer a cupcake sticker with two pieces of cardstock and adhere the piece to the card.

3. Write a message with a pink marker on a small strip of paper.

4. Use the marker to trace around the matted cupcake twice.

5. Use a hole punch and eyelet setter to attach the message with two eyelets.

Designer Sketch No. 10

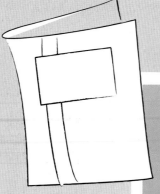

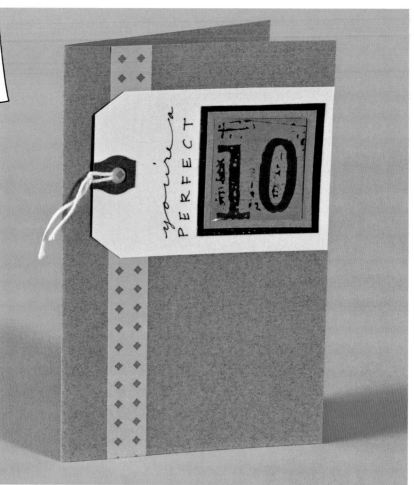

Example 1

1. Cut a small strip of decorative paper and glue it to the left-hand side of a green card.

2. Mount a number "10" epoxy sticker onto a piece of green cardstock and mat with brown decorative paper.

3. Adhere the matted sticker to a tag that has been trimmed in length to fit the card.

4. Add a message to the tag and adhere it to the card.

Example 2

1. Glue a piece of ribbon down the left side of the card.

2. Use pieces of cardstock and monogram rub-ons to decorate the top of the card.

3. Use a Micron pen to write the message and a binder clip to secure one of the letters.

Example 3

1. Adhere a strip of decorative tape to the left side of the card.

2. Cut and tear a piece of decorative paper for the focal point.

3. Embellish with a heart cut from decorative paper and a three-dimensional flower sticker.

Along with composition, we also use color every day.

Color can make us feel calm or excited, pleased or agitated. By giving color choice an important place in our lives—whether in the clothes we wear, the cards we make, or the meals we serve—we are personalizing our environment. I still remember my mom fussing over the color of the food on my dinner plate. It just wouldn't do to have white bread, cauliflower, and Fettuccine Alfredo in one meal!

A successful card design benefits as much from a good color combination as it does from a well-balanced composition. Many color combination ideas can be pulled from the world around us. A beautifully knitted, multicolored scarf or a set of brightly printed sheets could easily be the inspiration for a new card. The opposite is true, as well. A beautiful card can most definitely be the inspiration for a new outfit or set of throw pillows. If you find yourself in a design rut, try borrowing an intriguing color combination from your world. Another helpful idea is to save magazine clippings of pages that inspire you and keep a "color file" by your workspace.

This chapter's colorful path starts with the basics—a primer on primary, secondary, and tertiary colors. We'll then venture into the realm of color combinations bearing terms such as monochromatic, analogous, and triadic and discuss the use of hue (another word for color), tint, and shade, as well as how to think outside the card design box.

In the second half of the chapter, we'll walk you through pages of designer color swatches and give you three examples of how to create a pleasing design (and stunning card!) for each color combination.

PRIMARY COLORS

A lot of unfamiliar terms are used in the world of color—analogous, tertiary, triadic, for example— but it all begins with the three simple colors we call the primary colors: yellow, red, and blue. These colors are "primary," because you cannot create them by mixing other colors. If you are a parent, you might be familiar with the little crayon packs children get at restaurants, to color on their placemats. Those three primary colors start the color wheel a turnin'.

SECONDARY COLORS

When you place the primary colors evenly around the wheel, you'll find that you have space between each of them. This is where the secondary colors come in. Secondary colors are what you get when you mix two primary colors together: red and yellow to get orange ; blue and yellow to get green; and red and blue to get violet. These secondary colors, plus black and brown, make up the palette of an eight pack of crayons, an icon of childhood.

TERTIARY COLORS

Tertiary colors are created by mixing pairs of adjacent colors (one primary and one secondary) together. Now you get colors such as blue-violet, red-orange, blue-green, yellow-orange, red-violet, and yellow-green. The tertiary colors complete the basic color wheel, although you can continue to mix its colors to create even more colors. Tints and shades, which are discussed in the following section, can also be pulled from these colors.

TINTS, SHADES, AND SATURATION

Different colors have different values. (Value measures the lightness or darkness of a color.) Imagine writing on a poster with a yellow marker and a blue marker. Which color are you more likely to see from a distance? The yellow has a lighter value than the blue.

Each color can also have its own values, known as shades and tints. By adding white to a color, you create a tint. Adding white to red, for example, gives you pink, a tint. Adding black to a color gives you a shade. Add black to red, and you get brick red or maroon, which are shades of red. Tints and shades can be extremely helpful when choosing color schemes and infinitely increase your color combinations.

Saturation describes the brightness or intensity of a color. Adding gray to a hue lowers its saturation and creates a tone. A color's saturation is highest when the color is pure and lowers as gray or black is added to it.

TEMPERATURE

Colors have a perceived temperature. If you look at the color wheel, you'll see that it is divided into "warm" and "cool" colors. The warm side is made up of red, orange, and yellow colors, which evoke warmth of the sun and fire. Warm colors have a tendency to appear closer. If you need an element on a card to pop, consider using it in a warm color. Cool colors, such as blue, purple, and green, call to mind ice, water, and snow. Use cool colors in a design when you want something to recede.

Just to complicate things, some warm colors can have a cool cast (and vice versa). Take red, for example, which is notorious for causing color matching problems. A warm red can cast orange tones, while a cool red leans toward purple. Knowing to look for warm and cool casts in your design can help you keep paper and embellishments from clashing.

Cool colors

Warm colors

Color Schemes

Color schemes, those magical combinations of colors, have been studied by masters for hundreds of years. Each scheme offers a different way to use color in your card designs. Once a color scheme and colors have been chosen, carefully decide the amounts of each color you will use. A helpful analogy is to think of color use in "gallon, quart, and pint" measures. Use a "gallon" of your main color, a "quart" of another, and a "pint" of the third (and fourth). Using colors in this way allows the eye to settle on one element of the card at a time. Also consider shades, tints, and tones of a color when building your color scheme.

MONOCHROMATIC

The monochromatic color scheme uses just one color. Picasso's Blue Period, during which the artist painted primarily in blues and blue-green, was quintessentially monochromatic. Interspersing different shades, tints, and tones of a chosen hue adds interest to a design. Monochromatic schemes, which provide less contrast than multicolored combinations, tend to give a muted feel to a design and serve to create a particular mood. When using a monochromatic scheme, it can be difficult to highlight one particular element.

ANALOGOUS

Using a combination of three to five adjacent colors on the color wheel creates an analogous color scheme. Also a muted or subtle scheme, the analogous design can benefit from playing pure hues off shades and tints of the other hues in the scheme. Because the analogous scheme includes more colors, it can be richer than the monochromatic scheme. For a successful design, avoid using too many hues, and try to keep them either all warm or all cool.

COMPLEMENTARY

The complementary color scheme is one of my favorites. I use it all the time in my art, as well as in my daily life, and it never gets old. I once owned a little white Cape Cod–style house with blue shutters and always filled the window boxes with orange pansies and marigolds for an incredible "pop." There are a couple of things to keep in mind, however, when using a complementary color scheme. Complementary colors do not work well in a design if used in equal measures; employ the gallon, quart, pint method when using complementary colors. Be wary of the complementary colors of red and green—when used in their pure hues, they become reminiscent of the Christmas holiday. If you aren't making Christmas cards, try mixing one of the colors with a tint, shade, or tone of the other.

SPLIT COMPLEMENTARY

The split complementary color scheme uses one color and the two adjacent hues of its complementary color. Like the complementary scheme, the split complementary scheme offers great contrast. Unlike the complementary scheme, it does so without as much vibration between the colors, allowing the eye to see more distinction between them.

DOUBLE COMPLEMENTARY

Double your pleasure with a double complementary color scheme. You can create a colorful design using two sets of complementary colors. Remember to use different amounts of color, as well as tints, shades, and tones of each color.

TRIADIC

A triadic color scheme is achieved by using three colors spaced evenly along the color wheel. This scheme offers contrast while remaining balanced and harmonious.

Designer Swatch No. 1

Example 1

1. Cut a focal point from decorative paper, mat it, and then embellish it with a brass charm and ribbon.

2. Fold the card in an asymmetrical gatefold style, by making the right flap smaller than the left flap.

3. Use fine-gauge, black wire to spell out a message in a style that coordinates with the figures in the focal point. Attach the message by wrapping it around the edges and poking the ends into the spine, then securing them on the inside of the card.

Example 2

1. Use a scalloped square paper punch and a craft knife to create a buckle (downloadable template, Color Theory, Card #1), and thread it with two layers of cardstock.

2. Divide the card into two sections with striped and patterned decorative paper, then adhere the paper belt over the join, to "cinch" the card.

Example 3

1. Round the corners of the card and write the sentiment with a like-colored writing marker.

2. Color a rubber stamp with two co-ordinating markers and mist it lightly once with water, then stamp it three times onto paper.

3. Mount the paper onto decorative paper with rounded corners and attach a decorative binder clip to create a clipboard.

Designer Swatch No. 2

Baby Earth

Example 1

1. Mat polka-dot paper with brown paper trimmed with scallop edged scissors and adhere to a square card.

2. Use letter punches to cut the letters for the word "baby" from brown cardstock (punch small circles to create the insides of the letters), and adhere them along the bottom of a piece of yellow paper.

3. Attach the yelloaw baby piece to the card with blue imprinted ribbon.

Example 2

1. Apply strips of brown and decorative paper to the left-hand side of the card.

2. Attach delicate, die cut snowflakes to the right side.

3. Rubber stamp a message onto cardstock, mat it onto torn paper, and embellish it with eyelets.

4. Adhere the message with foam tape, for a sense of depth.

Example 3

1. Gatefold the card and embellish the touching edges with decorative map tape.

2. Insert six oversized, antique-style brads into the card, and lace them with a narrow ribbon.

3. Write the message on a coordinating tag (downloadable template, Color Theory, Card #2) and tie the tag to the top of the lacing.

Designer Swatch No. 3

Example 1

1. Tear a piece of green decorative paper and adhere it to the front of a black card.

2. Stamp the shoe pattern onto white cardstock and lightly rub ink around the edges of the stamped piece.

3. Mat the piece on polka dot paper and white cardstock, and mount it onto the card.

4. Cut a strip of green decorative paper and cut the left edge with pinking shears. Adhere to the bottom right corner of the card.

5. Stamp sentiment onto a small strip of white cardstock and lightly distress the piece with ink.

6. Adhere the sentiment to the decorative strip and embellish with two rhinestone brads.

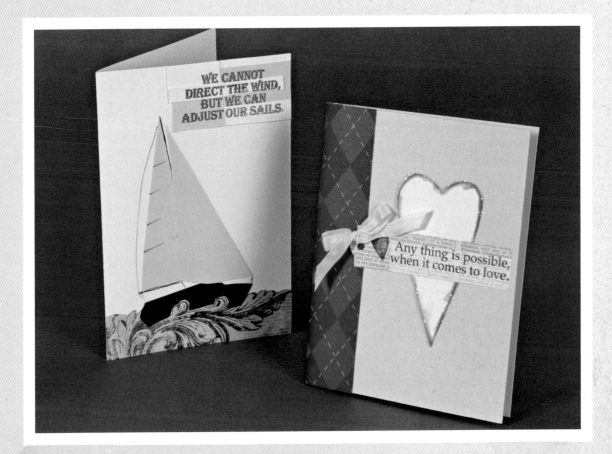

Example 2

1. Stamp the sentiment onto three colors of cardstock. Cut and layer to create a collage of words.

2. Cut out decorative paper to look like waves.

3. Cut out sail boat shape (downloadable template, Color Theory, Card #3).

4. Adhere the sailboat and wave paper to the card.

5. Use a Micron pen to add fine detail to the boat.

Example 3

1. Cut a strip of black decorative paper and attach it to the spine of the card.

2. Cut out a heart (downloadable template, Color Theory, Card #4) and edge it first with green ink and then with quick-dry tacky glue and glitter.

3. When dry, adhere the heart to the card and embellish it with a tag sticker and a ribbon.

Designer Swatch No. 4

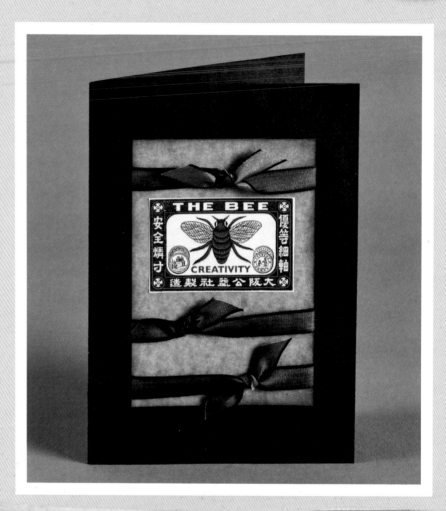

Example 1

1. Stamp bee image repeatedly onto brick-colored card in black and watermark ink.

2. Cut out bee focal point from decorative paper and glue to a piece of brown cardstock.

3. Lightly edge the brown cardstock with brown ink.

4. Tie three pieces of ribbon around the brown cardstock and adhere the piece to the card.

Example 2

1. Cut images from decorative paper and glue to a yellow card.

2. Use the Design Runner portable printer or a stamp to create a message along the bottom.

3. Cut two strips of decorative paper and adhere to each side of the message.

4. Glue a bow and key to the right side of the card.

Example 3

1. Stamp backgammon board image onto yellow cardstock and layer onto brick cardstock.

2. Glue backgammon piece to brown card and cut out the center opening using a craft knife.

3. Cut a piece of cardstock to fit the opening, and use a corner rounder punch to round the corners on one end, forming a tag.

4. Add a square reinforcement and an eyelet to the rounded end of the tag, and stamp it with the message.

5. Tie a ribbon through the eyelet and use foam tape to adhere the tag though the opening onto the inside of the card.

Designer Swatch No. 5

Spring Sampler

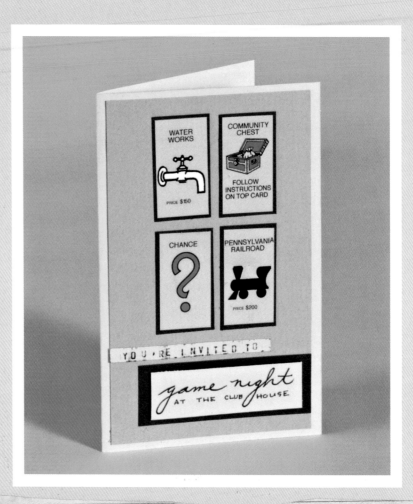

Example 1

1. Cut a large blue layer and adhere it to a light green card.

2. Write sentiment on light green cardstock (or use Design Runner) and mount onto a blue mat with foam tape. Adhere to the bottom of the card.

3. Cut a narrow strip of green paper, insert it into a label maker, and type out the rest of the message.

4. Run an ink pad lightly over the raised letters created by the label maker, and then glue the piece to the card.

5. Cut game pictures from themed decorative paper, mat, and adhere them to the card.

Example 2

1. Cut a piece of large-scale flower paper and adhere it onto a blue card.

2. Cut a strip of vellum paper and stamp it with the message.

3. Dip four brads into quick-dry tacky glue and then into glitter. Let dry.

4. Use an awl to poke holes into the card, and attach the vellum to the card with the brads.

Example 3

1. Fold a card just slightly off center to create an asymmetrical gatefold card.

2. Layer a narrow strip of decorative paper onto a wide strip and wrap it around the card.

3. Punch an oval from dark blue cardstock and mat it onto light blue cardstock. Cut around the oval with jumbo, scallop edge scissors.

4. Punch five flowers from coordinating decorative paper and attach them to the oval with decorative pearl brads (if necessary, use an awl to poke the holes).

5. Cut a fun tag and reinforcement (downloadable template, Color Theory, Card #5) and tie it with twine.

6. Adhere the tag to the oval and glue the oval to one side of the card front, so that it overlaps the join but still allows the card to open.

Designer Swatch No. 6

Example 1

1. Cover half of a tan card with striped decorative paper.

2. Create a "belt" for the card by layering narrow strips of decorative paper, and adhere it to the card.

3. Adhere a tan piece of cardstock onto a piece of decorative paper matted with blue cardstock, placing the tan piece off-center.

4. Cut a branch (downloadable template, Color Theory, Card #6) from blue paper and adhere it to the card.

5. Add a hummingbird sticker to the branch.

6. Add a fine line of quick-dry tacky glue to the edge of the hummingbird and add glitter.

Example 2

1. Cut a piece of decorative paper to fit the front of a brown card, and crumple it.

2. Add rub-ons to the paper and adhere it to the card.

3. Add two strips of decorative, text-printed tape.

4. Staple the tops and bottoms of the tape strips, to add texture.

5. Add another rub-on over the paper, tape, and card, to unify the design.

6. Cut a piece of paper to fit a label holder, and insert a decorative flower brad into the paper.

7. Attach the label holder and flower label to the card with brads. (If necessary, use an awl to poke holes.)

Example 3

1. Color a fish stamp with blue, tan, and brown markers and mist with water before stamping onto a blue card. Repeat multiple times.

2. Color a sentiment stamp with a brown marker and mist with water before stamping onto tan cardstock.

3. Mat the sentiment onto brown paper and adhere the piece to the bottom of the card with foam tape.

4. Wrap waxed twine three times around the top of the card and tie in a bow.

5. Cut a small tag (downloadable template, Color Theory, Card #7) and embellish it with a stamped piece of blue cardstock.

6. Use 18-gauge copper wire to make a small fishing hook.

7. Tie the hook and tag onto the string at the top of the card.

Designer Swatch No. 7

Example 1

1. Cut a piece of striped paper and adhere it to the left half of a red card.

2. Stamp the message along the right side of the card in red ink.

3. Stamp the focal point onto yellow cardstock in red ink.

4. Use quick-dry tacky glue to add glitter to the edge of the card and to highlight areas of the image. When dry, adhere the piece to the card with foam tape.

Example 2

1. Cut a wide strip of decorative paper and adhere it to a yellow card.

2. Cut a piece of vellum to layer onto the decorative paper and adhere it with vellum tape.

3. Cut flowers and brackets (download-able templates, Color Theory, Card #8) from coordinating cardstock and adhere them to the vellum with brads and glue.

4. Embellish with glitter, if desired.

5. Add floral brads.

6. Stamp the message along the bottom.

Example 3

1. Cut a strip of striped paper and adhere it to a pink card, along the spine.

2. Punch several button shapes into red and yellow cardstock.

3. Line up an upside-down, large circle punch over some of the button shapes and punch out, to create large paper buttons. Repeat with a small circle punch and a flower punch, to create small and flower-shaped paper buttons.

4. Adhere the buttons to the card.

5. Punch a button shape into a yellow cardstock rectangle and add a mes-sage around it with a marker.

6. Add an orange mat to the message and cut the edge with pinking shears.

7. Embellish the piece with button brads, and adhere the message to the card with foam tape.

Designer Swatch No. 8

Victorian Values

Example 1

1. Stamp party hat multiple times on sage green cardstock.
2. Color the hats with purple water-color paint and a silver metallic pen.
3. Tear and cut the party hat paper and adhere to purple decorative cardstock card, lining the paper up along the spine.
4. Stamp the message onto peach cardstock and edge with the silver metallic pen.
5. Adhere the message to the card.

Example 2

1. Cut and tear a piece of decorative paper and glue onto a peach card.

2. Stamp mother and daughter image onto ledger paper, then overstamp the image with a large shadow stamp inked in purple.

3. Trim the image and mat onto purple cardstock.

4. Adhere a pre-made bow to the card, then adhere the matted image over the bow with foam tape.

Example 3

1. Tear a piece of decorative paper and adhere to a sage green card. Repeat with a slightly smaller piece of peach cardstock.

2. Stamp the message onto the peach cardstock.

3. Punch two high-heeled shoes from purple cardstock and use a small sponge to ink the edges lightly.

4. Embellish the shoes with pearl stickers.

5. Glue one shoe onto the card, and adhere the second one with foam tape, slightly overlapping the other shoe, for dimension.

Designer Swatch No. 9

Example 1

1. Adhere a strip of torn paper to the left side of a green card.

2. Embellish the card with coordinating circle, tag, and strip stickers.

3. Add a striped ribbon to the top of the card and tie in a bow.

Example 2

1. Stamp the sentiment on a piece of decorative lined paper and glue it onto a blue card.

2. Use a hole punch and an eyelet setter to add six eyelets to the right side of the card.

3. Cut a heart from red polka-dot paper and mat it onto green paper.

4. Add a heart eyelet to the paper heart.

5. Lace the card eyelets with red waxed twine, threading twine through the eyelet of the paper heart.

Example 3

1. Tear a strip from the right side of a red card front, then adhere a piece of green cardstock underneath the front of the card.

2. Cut a piece of decorative paper and glue it to the left side of the card.

3. Cut out a number "1" (downloadable template, Color Theory, Card #9), trace around it with a Micron pen, tie a ribbon around it, and adhere it to the card with foam tape.

4. Use the Micron pen to add the message.

Designer Swatch No. 10

Alluring Aquatics

Example 1

1. Cut a piece of striped paper to fit an acrylic frame sticker.

2. Adhere the acrylic frame to the striped paper, adhere a photo in the opening, then adhere the frame to the card.

3. Stamp the skis onto a piece of teal cardstock and emboss.

4. Tear the edge and glue the piece to the card.

5. Using a white matte Glaze pen, write the message on a strip of torn paper.

6. When dry, glue the piece to the card.

7. Embellish the card with snow-flakes cut with a craft punch.

Example 2

1. Cut a piece of white cardstock and adhere it to a teal card.

2. Stamp Asian text on six squares of coordinating cardstock.

3. Adhere the pieces onto the card.

4. Stamp the focal point onto white cardstock and mount it with foam tape onto a piece of teal cardstock that has been torn and tied with a ribbon.

5. Adhere the focal point to the card.

Example 3

1. Stamp a pig in teal ink onto off-white cardstock.

2. Stamp the message below the pig with alphabet stamps.

3. Mat the piece with light green paper and adhere it to an off-white card.

4. Tie a bow with teal velvet ribbon and glue it onto the pig's neck.

Construction Studies

I love altering my point of view, especially when I'm working on cards.

These little canvases open and close, turn and flip, pop-up and pull out. Each card invites us to think differently, to try something new. On the following pages, we will play with many different constructions. Each card starts with a designer's model, which is replicated in three inspiring variations. You can use the models to make your cards or invent new designs that are all your own.

Designer Model No. 1

Small composition books with sewn-in pages are disassembled to create these unique and sturdy cards.

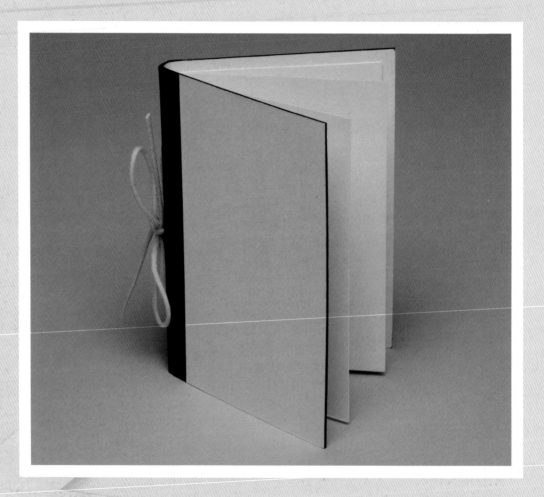

1. Use a craft knife to remove the pages from the composition books, and set them aside for another use.

2. Cover the front and back of the book with decorative paper and trim them to size with a craft knife.

3. Color the edges of the book with a marker to hide the cardboard color.

4. Cut one or two pieces of paper just smaller than the size of the opened cover.

5. Fold the paper in half and place it inside the cover.

6. Use a paper awl to punch three evenly spaced holes in the spine, and lace with ribbon, waxed twine, or other fiber.

7. Embellish as desired.

From the choice of binding to the cover embellishment, each of these cards is uniquely decorated.

i love you.

Black Card

Narrow black and white cording is used to lace this card, and paper stickers echo its composition book past.

Heart Card

This card was made using waxed thread, decorative-edge scissors, and different portions of the same decorative paper, which give it a coordinated look.

Package Card

The focal point of this card (downloadable template, Construction Study, Card #1) is a large representation of the elements in the decorative paper.coordinated look.

Heart Card, Package Card

Leave the inside pages of the card plain for writing a long message, or embellish them with a pocket (downloadable template, Construction Study, Card #2) to hold a gift card.

Black Card

Page tab embellishments make this card a real page-turner. To get even tabs, place the first one on at the top of the first page and the last one on the bottom of the last page, then carefully space out the remaining tabs on the middle pages.

Matchbook Cards

1. Cut a piece of cardstock a little more than twice as long as you want your card to be.

2. Cut an inside page (or pages) slightly smaller than the size of your finished card.

3. Fold up the bottom flap of the long piece of cardstock (make the fold at least ½" [1.75cm]), then slide the inside page(s) between the fold and the cardstock back.

4. Secure the flap with staples, brads, eyelets, or snaps, being sure to go through all the layers.

5. If you use multiple pages or thick embellishments on the inside pages, you'll need to create a small spine at the top of the card. To do this, score two narrowly spaced lines across the top of the card just above where the inside pages end. Fold the back of the card at the score lines and insert it into the bottom flap.

6. Embellish as desired.

From elegant wishes to construction inspired, each of these cards is strikingly different.

New home

The best part about writing this message is being able to draw guidelines with pencil, just like an architect! Snaps in the shape of screws are one of the construction touches, along with a stamped ruler and blueprint decorative paper.

A Mother Holds

This gentle card option combines a soft message, delicate layers of paper, and a glazed, punched heart. The bottom flap is cut with scallop edge scissors to give it a child-friendly aspect.

Good Luck

With careful scoring, it's relatively easy to use clear, printed acetate as a matchbook cover. Eyelets were added to attach a metallic bow.

Good Luck

Under the acetate is a foil shamrock and a message that has been stamped and embossed with gold powder.

A Mother Holds

Multiple layers on the inside exude extravagance.

From elegant wishes to construction inspired, each of these cards is strikingly different.

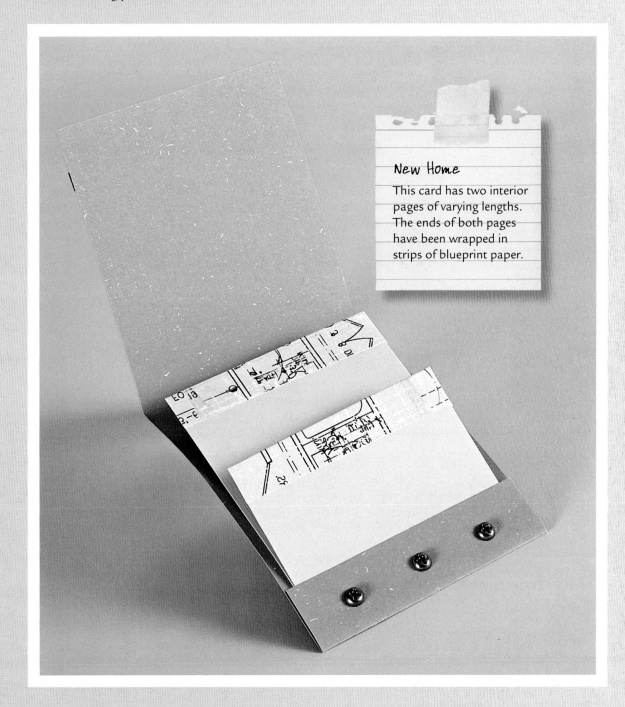

New Home
This card has two interior pages of varying lengths. The ends of both pages have been wrapped in strips of blueprint paper.

Designer Model No. 3

These cards are so much fun to open, and they're easy to create, once you know the secret.

You can adjust the size and the number of panels, but for the basic card, you will need four center panels that are at least 1" (2.5 cm) wide.

1. To create this card, fold a long piece of paper in half, and then make two score marks on each side of the center fold.

2. Fold along the score lines, then set the card on the table in front of you, so that you see three valley folds and two mountain folds.

3. Measure the front panel of your card and cut two pieces of cardstock ½" (1.25 cm) smaller than this measurement.

4. Cut the pieces horizontally into three even panels.

5. Adhere a panel to the top of the left side of the first mountain fold.

6. Adhere a second panel to the top, left side of the next mountain fold, so that the panels line up.

7. Adhere another panel to the middle of the right side of the first mountain fold. (It will face the opposite direction.)

8. Repeat, placing the next panel at the middle of the right side of the second mountain fold.

9. Adhere the last two panels to the bottom of the left side of the first and second mountain folds, as you did with the first two panels.

10. Embellish as desired.

Each of these cards—from a Halloween card to a lovely engagement card—uses the panels to customize its purpose.

8 is Great

A big, bold embossed "8" gives a little hint to what is inside of this card.

Bats

A window punched into the top of this skinny, spooky card reveals the uniquely shaped panels inside.

Flower

A delicate flower (downloadable template, Construction Study, Card #3) cut from off-white cardstock is shaped and glittered, then adhered to the card with foam dots.

8 is Great

Stamp four panels on the right side and two panels on the left side, so that all of the "8"s are seen. Stamp and emboss a bright, cheery message and adhere to inside back of the card.

Bats

Instead of cutting plain rectangular panels, cut bats from black cardstock and adhere them as described [directional]. Create additional folds, so that more bats can be added.

Flower

In this card, each panel carries one word of the inside sentiment, which is written with a matte Glaze gel pen. A matted piece of cardstock glued to the inside back of the card provides a place to write a special message.

Designer Model No. 4

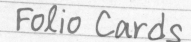

Folio Cards

This is not your average card. Inside are two pockets for adding that little something extra, such as theater tickets, a gift certificate, or maybe a special photo. The main card can be made from a sheet of scrapbook paper and some scraps.

1. Cut a piece of square scrapbook cardstock in half (perpendicular to the grain)

2. To make a spine, cut a strip of cardstock the height of card by your desired width.

3. Fold the spine in half and then open it back up and cover it with glue from a glue stick.

4. Place one half of the cardstock onto the glued spine, almost up to the fold.

5. Repeat with the other half of the cardstock.

6. Fold the left side of the cardstock piece in half, so that the edge almost touches the spine.

7. Open this back up, then fold over the top half of the outer section of the card diagonally, to create a triangle pocket. Secure the pocket in place with glue.

8. Close the card. You should now have a square card front and a long rectangular card back.

9. Fold the back piece of the card over the front, leaving a little space at the fold, so that the card opens easily.

10. Open the fold back up, then fold this last section in half, to create a narrow panel.

11. Open this section up one more time, and fold the upper right corner in on a diagonal to create a pocket. Secure the pocket with glue.

12. Punch a hole halfway down the spine and another halfway down the fold between the back panel and the right-hand pocket.

13. Thread a piece of ribbon through the holes to tie the folio shut.

14. If desired, cover the ribbon on the inside with a piece of cardstock.

Although these cards are all made using the same construction, they are very different in design.

Asian

With its floral wrap, this card evokes a Kimono.

Candy Cane

Bright and sweet, this card packs a holiday punch.

Rainbow

This card is a good example of repetition of color. The rainbow ribbon matches the flowers, which were stamped using a rainbow ink pad.

Asian

The right-hand panel of this card is folded in on itself vertically, to create a long, slim pocket. The inside card is tied with waxed twine, decorated with a matted stamped image, and adhered to the outside card. A piece of matted cardstock is slipped into the left-hand pocket.

Rainbow

The inside cardstock panel was stamped with rainbow flowers and a sentiment and matted onto decorative paper. The bright cardstock pops against the kraft paper and soft rainbow hues.

Candy Cane

Before adhering the cardstock over the ribbon on the inside, it was layered onto decorative paper and then embellished with a candy cane cut from the extra paper. The right panel isn't needed as a pocket, so both the bottom and top corners were folded in, to create symmetry.

Designer Model No. 5

This card is deceptively easy to make and, as you will see in the examples, is fun to alter for any occasion. Two pieces of cardstock, four simple folds, and a little glue are all that are needed to create this nifty, interactive card.

1. Cut two identically sized rectangles of cardstock, one for the inside of the card, one for the outside.

2. Fold the outside piece of cardstock in half, to create the cover for the card.

3. With the right side facing out, fold the inside piece of cardstock in half.

4. Fold the right and left sides of this piece of cardstock back to the center fold, creating a center mountain fold and two valley folds.

5. Adhere the two outer flaps of the inside piece to the cover of the card, making sure to match the outside edges.

6. Embellish as desired.

These three cards are hip, romantic, and graphic in their own particular designs.

Wild Thing

The graphic bulls-eye spine adds a hip twist to this pop-up card. The message is hand written with a matte Glaze gel pen, but it can also be easily stamped and embossed.

Love

An embossed sentiment is matted onto card-stock and embellished with graduated pearl stickers. A piece of leaf cut from the spare card-stock is mounted with the sentiment and a pre-made bow to the cover of the card.

Hugs

Two holes are punched into the spine of this card and tied with printed ribbon. The sentiment is stamped, double matted, and embellished with snaps that mimic the dots on the decorative paper.

Hugs

1. To create the inside sentiment, use a tag punch to cut out eight tags.

2. Adhere four x's and four o's cut with a die cutting tool to the tags.

3. Use a hole punch and eyelet setter to add eyelets to the tags, and adhere the tags to the card with foam tape.

Wild Thing

Two-sided decorative cardstock is used on this eye-popping card.

1. To make the card, cut the heart out of the center piece while it is still folded but before it is glued to the cover.

2. Add a message with a matte Glaze gel pen (or stamp and emboss the message).

Love

1. To create this pop-up within a pop-up, make two 1" (2.5 cm) horizontal slits through the center fold of the inside piece.

2. Fold the section between the slits back and forth, to make a crease.

3. Cut two more ½" slits between the first two slits to make the smaller pop-up and bend back and forth, to make a crease.

4. Push the larger section into the card and, from behind, push the smaller pop-up forward.

5. To make the two lovely rings, use two die cut letter o's set onto their sides. Adhere them to the smaller pop up.

6. Use a rhinestone embellishment for a diamond.

Supply Inspiration

Welcome to the chapter that cures all creative blocks!

I like to think of supply inspiration as my creative muse. When I am stuck for an idea, uninspired to create, or just ready for something new, I turn to my supplies. Of course, it helps that I'm a bit of a collector. Because I am also a fine artist, I have a studio full of found treasures, old photographs, vintage bottles, and even an old violin. Some of these bits and pieces make it into my card designs (and some obviously don't), but I like to wander through my little treasures, looking for inspiration.

In this chapter, I use readily available supplies and embellishments, such as rubber stamps, decorative scissors, and even die cuts. By delving into my supplies, I either come up with new ideas or force myself to start a project by enticing my inner penny pincher to make use of an underutilized supply.

Each supply item is shown used in multiple ways—a frugal designer's dream. Try pulling out that stamp you just had to have and use it. Or rummage through the scrap papers you couldn't bear to part with and create something new!

Designer Supply No. 1

Working with stamps offers ample opportunity to make multiple cards without using endless supplies. They are also extremely versatile. You can use one stamp to create a background, a focal point, or an embellished accent. The possibilities are almost endless.

Example 1

This petal envelope holds a flat panel card, which is stamped with a message and embossed in a green iridescent powder before being matted multiple times.

1. To make the spoon accent, first create a mask by stamping the spoon image onto a sticky note and cutting it out.

2. Use a cosmetic sponge to apply ink over the mask, to create a silhouette.

3. Use a stamp aligner to stamp the image directly over the silhouette.

4. For an added embellishment, adhere a ribbon to the card below the spoon.

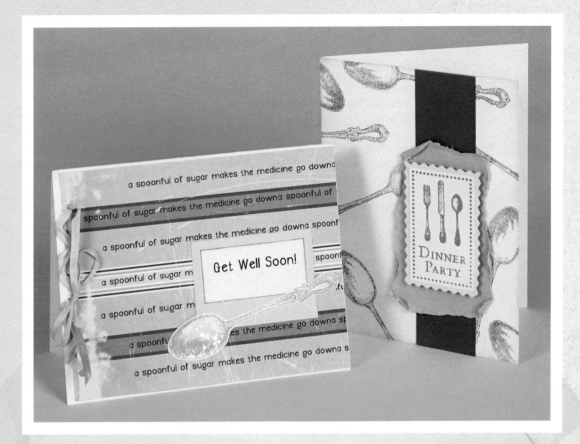

Example 2

1. Use the Design Runner to print a design multiple times on decorative paper.

2. Cut out the image and adhere it onto the card.

3. Punch five holes into the left edge of the card and lace them with silk ribbon.

4. With the Design Runner, print "Get Well Soon!" onto a piece of cardstock edged with ink and matted on the bottom right corner of the card.

5. Stamp the image, emboss it with iridescent silver powder, and cut it out.

6. Apply glue to the bowl of the spoon and sprinkle it with vintage glass glitter, to create "sugar."

7. Adhere the spoon onto the message.

Example 3

1. Stamp the spoon image multiple times to create a decorative paper background.

2. Adhere a strip of paper to the front right side of the paper and layer it with a torn and slightly distressed piece of cardstock.

3. The focal point (dinner party image) is stamped onto matching paper, layered onto a piece of paper cut with pinking shears, and attached to the card with foam tape.

Designer Supply No. 2

Ribbon is one of my favorite supplies. I especially love gingham and polka-dot varieties. Ribbon can be used for a closure, a decorative bow, or even something utilitarian, such as photo corners.

Example 1

1. Fold a piece of gray cardstock into a gatefold card.

2. Randomly stamp the image onto the card front, first with dye ink, and then with pigment ink.

3. Emboss the pigment ink images using embossing powder and a heat gun.

4. Punch a hole in each side of the card and thread the ribbon through the holes.

5. Attach a matching stamped and embossed message tag to the ribbon before tying the card shut with a bow.

Example 2

1. Stamp a green card randomly with a leaf image in clear embossing ink.

2. Sprinkle three different embossing powders on the leaves, tap off the excess, and emboss.

3. Stamp and emboss the sentiment with the excess mixed powders.

4. Mat the sentiment and mount it onto the card, using ribbon as photo corners.

5. Use a craft punch to punch a leaf shape.

6. Apply quick-dry tacky glue to the surface of the leaf, and sprinkle it with small amounts of mica powder and glitter.

7. Adhere the glittered leaf to the card with a foam dot.

Example 3

1. Adhere a large piece of torn decorative paper to the front of a pink card.

2. Stamp a balloon image onto pink cardstock and cut out the image.

3. Adhere the balloon and a tied bow to the card with foam tape and glue.

4. Stamp "Hope" on a small piece of cardstock and double mat it before adhering it to the card.

Designer Model No. 3

Although some punches are theme oriented and their use limited, others, such as this scalloped circle, come in handy over and over again. Here, I've used the punch as a window maker, a decorative element, and a utilitarian page tab.

Example 1

1. Add a rub-on message to a piece of decorative cardstock, and trim the corners with a corner rounder punch.

2. Mat the message twice, rounding the corners.

3. Adhere the message to a strip of teal paper mounted across the top portion of the card.

4. Punch out a gold scalloped circle and a larger teal circle, and create a "number 1" ribbon using ribbon, a rub-on, and foam tape.

5. Adhere the ribbon to the card.

Example 2

1. Cut and tear a piece of decorative paper to fit the front of a square card.

2. Embellish the card with coordinating rub-ons.

3. Attach a square piece of vellum over the card with staples.

4. Adhere a sentiment sticker onto a piece of red paper, and add it to the card with foam tape.

5. Add a rub-on below the sentiment.

6. Punch two scalloped circles from brown paper, and insert a bird shaped brad through one of the circles.

7. Create a page tab by sandwiching the upper edge of the card between the circles.

Example 3

1. Use a craft punch to cut a window in the lower right hand side of the card.

2. Place a sticker inside the card, so that it shows through the opening.

3. Randomly embellish the front of the card with rub-ons.

4. Add a message sticker along the bottom of the card, along with one final rub-on underneath the window.

Designer Model No. 4

These innocent looking pens are my secret weapon. I use them on everything, including my fine art. In these examples, I use them for drawing, detailing, and even hand lettering. They come in multiple sizes, and I use them all.

Example 1

1. On a gray card, doodle swirls and little circles with Micron pens in three sizes.

2. Stamp a leaf in watermark ink on light gray cardstock, and rub with mica powder to get a subtle distressed look.

3. Mat the leaf onto black cardstock, and punch two holes in the side of the piece.

4. Tie ribbon through the holes and mount the piece to the card with foam tape.

Example 2

1. Cut a house shape from orange paper and door and window shapes (downloadable template, Supply Inspiration, Card #1) from gray paper. Adhere the door and window to the house and mount the house on a gray card.

2. Outline the house twice, with two pen sizes.

3. Outline the door and windows once.

4. Write "We've moved" underneath the house.

Example 3

1. Ink a background stamp with a rainbow ink pad and spritz with water before stamping onto yellow cardstock.

2. Mount the stamped image onto black cardstock and adhere the piece to the card.

3. Hand letter the sentiment (use a pencil first, if desired) on yellow cardstock and embellish it with small dots.

4. Mat the sentiment three times and adhere it to the card with foam tape.

Designer Supply No. 5

Working successfully with decorative scissors can be tricky, but you won't go wrong if you stick with some basic pairs. I have many pairs of decorative scissors, but my pinking shears and scallop edge scissors (in multiple sizes) get the most use. I used pinking shears to create a decorative mat, a fun card edge, and a piece of paper rickrack for these cards.

Example 1

1. Cut and tear a piece of decorative paper to fit on a black card.

2. Mat the paper and adhere it to the card.

3. Stamp a chessboard image onto tan cardstock and cut it out.

4. Adhere the chessboard to a piece of black cardstock, and trim around the edge of the cardstock with pinking scissors.

5. Adhere the chessboard piece to the card.

6. Cut a strip of black cardstock, and poke four holes down each side.

7. Lace the holes randomly with waxed twine.

8. Use a craft punch to punch out a tag.

9. Stamp a chess figure onto the tag and emboss it.

10. Use a hole punch and eyelet setter to add an eyelet.

11. Add the tag to the lacing and tie the lacing into a bow.

Example 2

1. Cut a strip of paper rickrack with pinking scissors and adhere it to the bottom of a yellow card.

2. Punch a flower from orange cardstock and adhere it to the card.

3. With a Micron pen, write the message underneath the flower.

Example 3

1. Cut the road and landscape (downloadable template, Supply Inspiration, Card #2) from gray and green cardstocks, and adhere them to a light blue card.

2. Draw lane markers on the road with a matte Glaze gel pen, and add a car sticker.

3. Stamp the message on light blue cardstock, mat it with teal cardstock, and adhere it to the card with foam tape.

4. Embellish the message with a horn sticker.

Designer Supply No. 6

I love organization. I love cubbies, small boxes, and especially label holders. Attached to a card, these little label holders do more than their original utilitarian job. A label holder can serve as a photo frame, a window, and as a way to spell out a message—very versatile.

Example 1

1. Mount a label holder onto the bottom right corner of a lavender card.

2. Cut a small photo to fit into the label holder and secure into place with adhesive.

3. Stamp the message in purple ink above the photo.

Example 2

1. Cut and tear a strip of decorative paper to fit the center of a gray card.

2. Mount three label holders down the middle of a piece of gray cardstock.

3. Use alphabet stamps to stamp out the message and insert the pieces into the label holders.

4. Mat this piece with a larger piece of off-white cardstock.

5. Add a message with a Micron pen and adhere the piece to the card.

Example 3

1. Tear a strip of paper to fit across a brown card.

2. Stamp a message on the strip and adhere it to the card.

3. Place a label holder onto the card and trace the opening.

4. Remove the label holder and cut out the opening with a craft knife and a cutting mat.

5. Mount the label holder over the opening and place a three-dimensional sticker inside the card, so that it shows through the window.

Designer Supply No. 7

Sometimes it's fun to step away from your everyday card making supplies and try something new. Wire is definitely one of the more interesting supplies to use on cards. Employing wire to make custom paper clips, miniature spiral binding, and spelled out messages can really make a card shine.

Working with Wire

Example 1

1. Tear a piece of light gray paper, distress the edges with gray ink, and adhere it to the card.

2. Stamp beverage labels onto cardstock, cut them out, and adhere them to the card.

3. To make the wire paper clip, cut a length of wire with a wire cutter and use needle nose pliers to turn the wire into a spiral.

4. Attach the paper clip to the card.

5. Add staples to one of the labels.

Example 2

1. Cut a long length of wire and wrap it tightly around a round dowel.

2. Remove the wire from the dowel and carefully pull it apart, evenly separating the spirals.

3. Stamp a sentiment and temporarily tack it into place on the bottom left corner of a light blue card.

4. Place the wire binding along the edge of the card and mark the placement of the spirals.

5. Remove the binding and punch $\frac{1}{16}$" holes at each marking. Be sure to punch through the card and the sentiment.

6. Gently ease the wire binding through the holes, and tie short lengths of ribbon to it.

7. Stamp the main image onto white paper and color it with watercolors or watercolor pencils.

8. Mat the image onto a cut and torn piece of green cardstock and affix it to the card with staples.

Example 3

1. Stamp the background image in clear embossing ink and emboss with clear embossing powder.

2. Cut a length of wire and carefully shape into a word. This is just like writing in cursive.

3. Use quick-dry tacky glue to adhere the word to the card, and embellish with a copper brad, if desired.

4. Tie a ribbon along the top of the card.

Designer Model No. 8

Almost all of the cards in this book use decorative paper, and, although the whole is said to be greater than the sum of the parts, decorative paper has many useful parts! It can be successfully cut apart to provide a main feature, a background, a mat, and even a lining.

Example 1

1. Cut a large blue square, mat it with decorative paper, and adhere it to a pink card.

2. Cut a strip of paper and dovetail the ends, so that it resembles a ribbon.

3. Stamp the message in the center of the strip and mat the strip with a piece of cardstock.

4. Fold in the ends of the stamped paper ribbon and adhere the ribbon to the card.

5. Cut flowers from the decorative paper.

6. Adhere some of the flowers to the card with a glue stick and some with foam dots.

Example 2

1. Line the inside cover of a card with decorative paper.

2. Bend the top right corner toward the front and secure it with three brads.

3. Stamp a message onto cardstock and double mat it with cardstock and decorative paper.

4. Adhere the message to the card and embellish it with photo turns and brads.

Example 3

1. Cut a large piece of decorative paper for the background and adhere it to a blue card.

2. Stamp a shoe image onto cardstock and cut it out.

3. Mount the shoe with foam tape to a matted piece of cardstock and adhere the piece to the card.

4. Stamp the message on a small piece of cardstock and trim two corners, to make it look like a tag.

5. Use a hole punch and an eyelet setting tool to add an eyelet to the tag.

6. Tie a piece of waxed twine around the spine and add the tag.

Designer Model No. 9

I use eyelets all the time. Very rarely will I punch a hole and not put an eyelet into it. For the most part, eyelets provide a finished look that makes the recipient wonder if the card is hand made or store bought. Eyelets can be used as reinforcements for paper tags, as a way to attach vellum to a card, or as decorative elements, such as those seen on the baby card.

Example 1

1. Cut and adhere a piece of decorative paper to a pink card.

2. Cut and tear a strip of pink cardstock, ink the edges, and adhere it to the bottom section of the card.

3. Add eyelets to three tag stickers, tie them with waxed twine, and adhere the tags to the card.

4. Add three heart stickers to the three tags.

Example 2

1. Attach a large sentiment sticker to a blue card.

2. Cut a large vellum square and attach it to the card with four eyelets, using a hole punch and an eyelet setting tool.

3. Add a cupcake sticker to the vellum piece.

Example 3

1. Cut and tear a piece of pink cardstock and attach it to a card made from decorative cardstock.

2. Add stitching and message rub-ons.

3. Use a die cut tool to cut a onesie.

4. Add extra-small eyelets to the snap holes on the die cut and adhere the piece to the card.

Designer Model No. 10

Many of the tools and supplies discussed in this section are relatively inexpensive, but the die cut machine is not. It is, however, addictively useful and fun to operate. This die cutting machine, made by Xyron, plugs into a computer. With a die cut machine like this, you can cut out entire cards, small elements, or special windows for your cards. (It has myriad other uses, as well.)

Example 1

1. Use die cutting software to draw a field of grasses, or download a design from *www.wishblade.com*.

2. Cut out the design with the machine.

3. Layer two pieces of cardstock onto an off-white card.

4. Adhere the die cut to the front of the card.

Example 2

1. Use the die cutting software to draw a menorah, or download a design from *www.wishblade.com.*

2. Use the software to position the menorah in the center of the card, and cut it out with the machine.

3. Cut a narrow strip of paper, spread it with glue, and sprinkle it with gold glitter.

4. Glue the strip to the back of the card front, behind the flames of the die cut opening.

5. Cut a large piece of off-white cardstock and glue it onto the inside of the card, to cover the rest of the menorah.

6. Use a large corner rounder to round the two right-hand corners.

Example 3

1. Use the die cutting software to draw two identical stars "welded" together to make a card.

2. Cut out the card with the machine.

3. Use the die cutting software to draw the sentiment, and cut it out with the machine.

4. Decorate the border of the card with a Micron pen and glitter.

6. Add glitter to the sentiment and glue it onto the card.

Working with Multiples

This chapter provides smart solutions for working in multiples.

The previous chapters may be wonderful resources for creating special cards for dear friends and family members, but what do you do if you need to make fifty Christmas cards, twenty thank you notes, or thirty-five bridal invitations? (Besides panic.) In this section, we'll ease your worries and talk about simplifying your designs and using an assembly line process so that you can work quickly to produce many paper masterpieces instead of just one or two. We'll also discuss "buying smart," and how purchasing products that come in multiples will help to create many duplicate cards for less.

When I find time in my studio, I enjoy making sets of cards to give as gifts. Sometimes these sets are a quick present that I bundle up with simple card wraps like those featured in this chapter. Even just four handmade cards and matching envelopes will make a great gift for a teacher or friend. For more involved stationery sets I like to make a portfolio like the one on page 136. This little beribboned case can hold many cards, envelopes, and even labels and stamps.

There is no need to fear when you have lots of cards to make; in fact, you may even decide to make multiples of all your projects so that you will always have a selection of cards to send.

Simplify

Nothing that can spoil a party, even before it starts, like a daunting pile of invitations that need to be created. Although you know that everyone will love the invite and save it for a long time, you just don't have time to make thirty works of art. This is the time to simplify. The card examples that follow are relatively similar to each other in design, but by slightly changing the process, tool, or supply, the time needed to create each card can be reduced significantly.

This card has a hand stamped spine, hand sewn detail, background paper cut with decorative scissors, and a hand written message attached with brads.

Ships are safe in harbor,
but that's not what
ships were made for.

This card uses printed paper instead of a hand stamped spine. Stitching drawn with matte Glaze gel pens replaces the hand sewn detail. Although cutting paper with decorative scissors is not overly time consuming, tearing the background paper is even faster. And finally, by stamping the message instead of hand writing it, and using staples in place of brads, this card is completed in much less time than the initial version, with approximately the same outcome.

In the early 1900s, Henry Ford created an improved assembly line, and the world was never the same. He was able to lower the cost of a Model T from $950 to less than $300 by saving production costs. Just think what you can accomplish by making multiple cards in assembly line style.

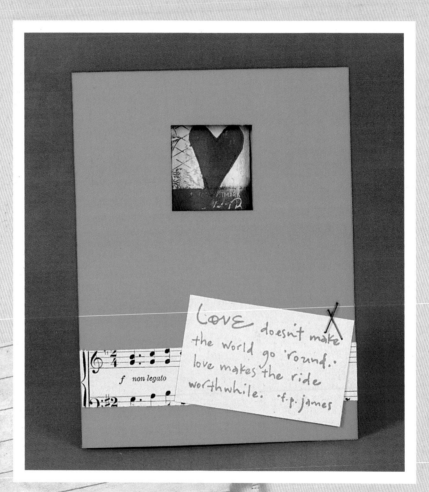

The first step in setting up an assembly line is to create a card that can be easily broken down into steps or processes. This card is a good example of an easy card to prep and assemble.

Buying Smart

One of the best ways to save time when you're creating multiple copies of the same card is to use premade embellishments. Unfortunately, the contents of a package of embellishments often consist of items that are all different. By choosing embellishment packages in which the items are the same or similar, such as the epoxy heart stickers used for this card, you can save considerable expense—and design headaches!

1. The cards are cut, folded, and punched with a square punch.

2. Sheet music is cut into strips.

3. The sentiment for the front of the card is stamped repeatedly, and then cut into pieces.

4. The cards are assembled, one step at a time.

A simple, sweet, and effective way to present a gift set of cards is to surround it with an elegant wrap. By cutting decorative paper, adding an embellishment, and wrapping it around a set of cards, you can easily create a stunning gift. For a more elaborate gift, make a card folio. By switching paper types, you can change the theme from bright and sunny to masculine or elegant. You can also embellish your wraps and folios to match the cards inside, if desired.

Card Wraps

1. Cut two strips of paper of different widths.
2. Use a glue stick to adhere the narrower strip to the wider one.
3. Wrap the paper around a set of cards and trim any excess.
4. Affix an epoxy sticker to a cardstock mat and adhere the piece to the wrap, hiding the join.

1. Cut two sets of narrow and wide paper strips.

2. Use a glue stick to adhere the narrower strips to the wider strips.

3. Wrap one set of strips around a set of cards, trimming any excess but leaving a little overlap.

4. Use a glue stick to glue the overlapping portions together.

5. Bend the second paper strip into a bow shape and cut off the extra length.

6. Wrap the extra length around the bow, to create a center knot, and glue the bow to the wrap.

This portfolio shines with simplicity and specialty ribbon. Try adding embellishments to match the cards on the inside. Don't forget to add a sheet of stamps for the lucky recipient.

Card Folios

1. Trace the folio template (download-able template, Card Folios, Card #1) onto the back of a piece of printed cardstock.

2. Score along the marked fold lines and punch the marked holes.

3. Thread ribbon through the holes.

4. Trace the endpaper template (down-loadable template, Card Folios, Card #2) onto coordinating scrapbook paper, and cut it out.

5. Fold in the right and left tabs on the top half of the folio, glue them down, and cover them with the endpaper.

6. To create the pockets, add glue to the outside edges of the right and left bottom tabs and fold the bottom section up.

7. Add cards and envelopes and tie shut.

30 REASONS TO SEND A CARD*

1. I'm Sorry
2. I'm NOT Sorry
3. Happy Birthday
4. New home
5. Thanksgiving
6. Valentine's Day
7. Happy Belated Anniversary
8. I Love You
9. I Like You
10. Good report card
11. New car
12. New dog
13. New therapist
14. Wedding (1st, 2nd, 3rd …)
15. Congrats on Your Divorce
16. Christmas
17. Rosh Hashanah
18. New Year's
19. Just because
20. Kwanzaa
21. Chanukah
22. Easter
23. Get Well Soon
24. Sorry I Crashed the Car
25. Groundhog's Day
26. New job
27. Thinking of You
28. Expecting
29. New baby
30. Hang in There

*This list is just a sampling of the most popular reasons to send a card. It does not include the lesser known occasions such as Puppy Obedience Training Graduation, Sorry about Your Splinter, and Thank You for Remembering to Pick Up the Dry Cleaning.

"And none will hear the postman's knock
without a quickening of the heart.
For who can bear to feel himself forgotten?"

—W.H. Auden

Ins & Outs

This chapter is the embodiment of two familiar adages.

The first is, "Never underestimate the power of a first impression." The sight of an envelope in the day's stack of mail that doesn't look like a bill is exhilarating. Whether you were expecting it (it's your birthday) or were caught by surprise (it was sent "just because"), you treasure the sentiment that much more when it comes in a pretty package. That package could be as simple as a store-bought envelope with a matching sticker on the back or as involved as a handmade and lined envelope. This chapter will walk you through the processes for creating a card from scratch, using an old envelope as a template, adding linings to your envelopes, and decorating the label area and envelope fronts to match.

The second adage is, "It's what's on the inside that counts." This is why the end of this chapter is filled with lovely, funny, and sincere sentiments that you can use in your own cards, when you don't know what to say. Some may even lead you to create cards you didn't know you wanted to send. Many of these sayings can be downloaded from the Internet.

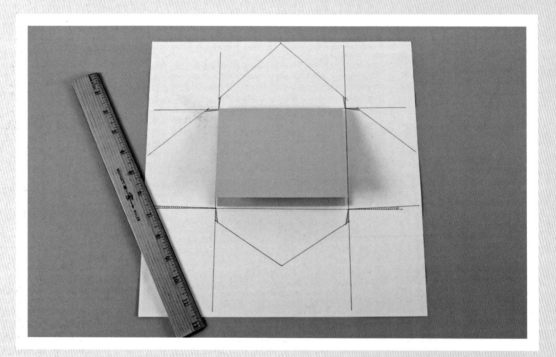

1. Place a card onto the center of a piece of scrap book paper. (Regular weight works best for this.)

2. Use a ruler and a pencil (a pen was used here to make the lines more visible) to make vertical and horizontal lines just outside the edges of the card. This defines the top, bottom and side flaps of your envelope.

3. Determine the height of the upper flap and make a mark at this point, at the center of the envelope.

4. Measure up approximately ½" (1.27 cm) on both of the bottom corners of the top flap and make a mark.

5. Draw a line from this point to the top center point.

6. Repeat this procedure to make the bottom flap.

7. To create the side flaps, measure ½" (1.27 cm) along the upper left edge of the right hand flap and make a mark.

8. Make a second mark half way down the right edge of the right hand flap.

9. Draw a diagonal line connecting these two points.

10. Repeat this procedure with the left hand flap.

11. To remove the excess bulk, so that the envelope folds smoothly, trim a small wedge off the sides of each flap, as shown in the photograph.

12. Cut out the envelope, fold it, and secure the flaps with glue, leaving the top flap open.

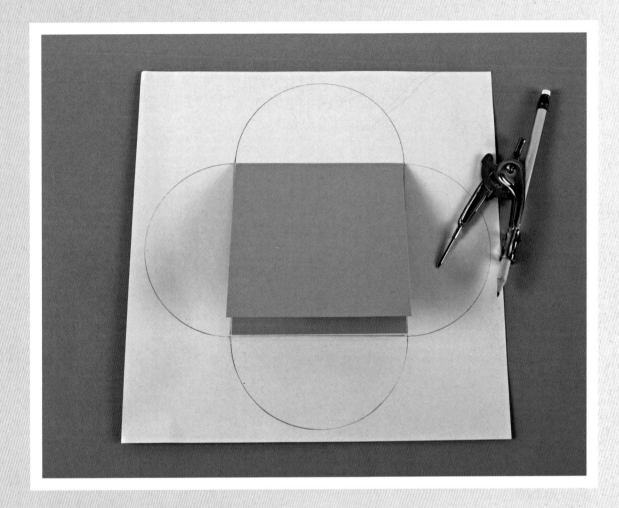

1. Place a square card in the center of a piece of cardstock. (Cardstock is better to use for this type of envelope.)

2. Use a pencil and a ruler to draw a light line just outside the edges of the card.

3. Use a plate, circle template, or compass to draw semicircles for each flap of the envelope.

4. Cut out along the outside edge of the envelope and fold the petals in.

5. To close the envelope, fold the petals in one at a time, inserting the last petal under the first to secure.

Numerous books, die cuts, and templates for tracing envelopes are available, but I find it incredibly handy to trace an old one! By opening up the glued edges of a used envelope (or a new one), you can trace the shape onto old magazine pages, calendar pages, scrapbook paper, decorative paper, or even newsprint. The possibilities are endlessly customizable and unique.

1. Open up an old envelope and trace it onto a piece of scrapbook paper.
2. Cut out along the edges.
3. Fold in each of the flaps, using a bone folder to get a crisp crease.

Shown above are the original envelope and the new envelope made from decorative paper using the manila file folder template. To add to its customized look, this envelope was also lined. See the next section for more information on how to line your envelopes.

An envelope lining is that extra-special touch that you can add to envelopes for special occasions or whenever the whim takes hold. An envelope lining can coordinate or complement and can be subtle or bold. The process is simple, requiring little more than a pencil, glue stick, and scissors.

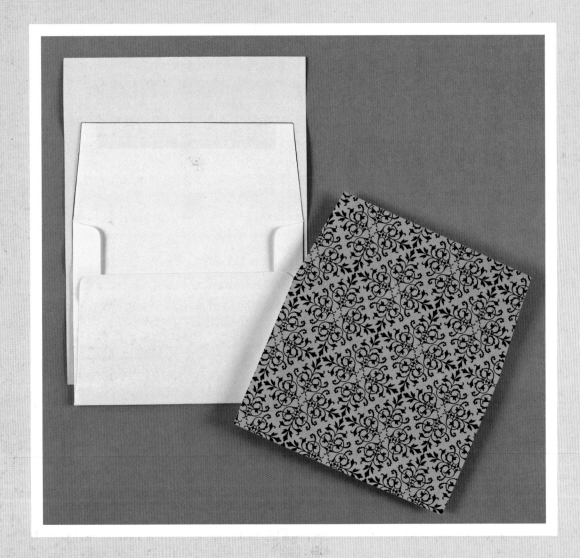

1. Lay the envelope to be lined onto the back of a piece of lining paper.

2. Line up the envelope, so that the bottom ½" (1.25 cm) extends off the bottom edge of the paper.

3. Trace around the envelope and cut the piece out, cutting just inside the tracing line.

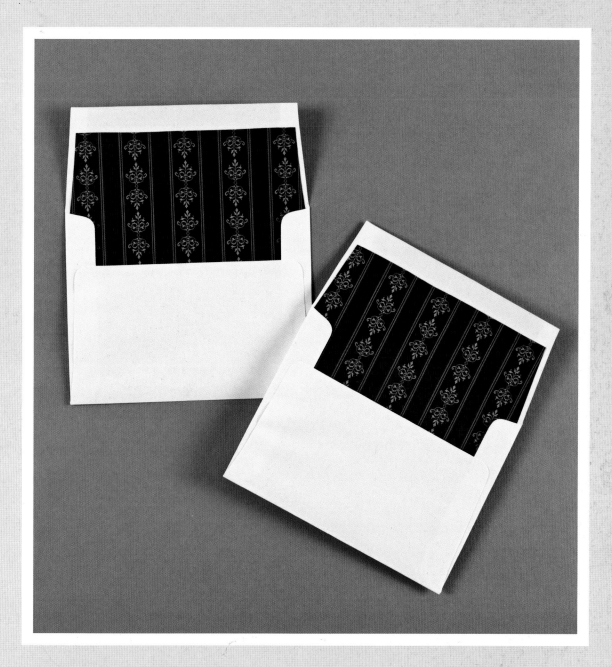

4. Slip the lining into the envelope.

5. Pull the top flap of the lining out of the way, and use a glue stick to glue the flap of the envelope.

6. Adhere the lining to the envelope.

7. Fold over the top flap of the envelope and crease it with a bone folder.

Envelopes of all shapes and sizes can be lined in fun and interesting ways to coordinate or complement accompanying cards.

Making Labels

Another special touch to add to a finished card is a decorated label. In these examples, the label area is highlighted by decorating around the address portion of the envelope.

Heart Envelope >

1. Cut strips of decorative stickers to create a frame around the label area of the envelope.
2. Embellish the bottom left corner with two stacked heart stickers.

< Flower Envelope

1. Cut a sticky note to label size and temporarily adhere it to the center of the envelope.
2. Ink a floral stamp with a rainbow ink pad and stamp the image onto the envelope.
3. Repeat around all four edges of the envelope, then remove the sticky note.

Green Envelope >

1. Cut a sticky note to label size and temporarily adhere it to the center of the envelope.
2. Use a small sponge dauber or make-up sponge pressed into a dye based ink pad to color around the edges of the sticky note. Press the dauber or sponge down onto the sticky note, then pull it off the edge of the note, lifting slightly as you move off the edge of the note.

Now that you've learned how to line envelopes and make labels, the obvious next step is to create a themed presentation. By coordinating the inside and outside of an envelope, you create the kind of panache that just isn't available in a store bought card. Noticed the minute they are taken out of the mailbox, these envelopes are often saved with the card! When you really want someone to know how much you care, start with the envelope and end with a beautiful card.

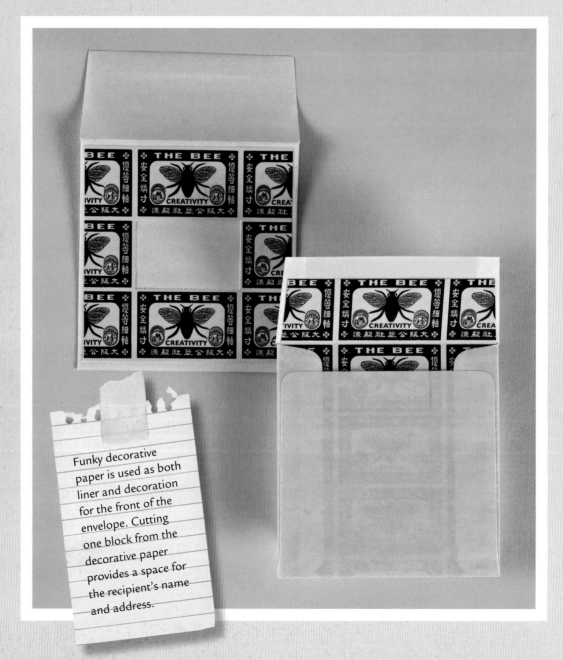

Funky decorative paper is used as both liner and decoration for the front of the envelope. Cutting one block from the decorative paper provides a space for the recipient's name and address.

The small strip of road along the front of this envelope provides a hint of its interior lining. An embossed car sticker adds a sense of whimsy.

The Right Thing To Say

The following collection of sentiments can be used on the inside or outside of a card. I gathered and arranged the quotes and sayings into like categories, but feel free to reword them and make them your own. Try substituting the word family for friends, for example, or father for mother, to create the perfect wording for your next card.

BIRTHDAY AND CELEBRATIONS

May you live all the years of your life.
—*Author Unknown*

May you live as long as you want.
And may you never want as long as you live.
—*An Irish Blessing*

It really would be wonderful
To be with you each day . .
To laugh with you,
And talk with you,
And pass the time away.
But since that isn't possible,
The next best thing to do
Is give this wish for
Happiness to last the
Whole year through.
—*Author Unknown*

We know we're getting old when the only thing we want for our birthday is not to be reminded of it.
—*Author Unknown*

There is still no cure for the common birthday.
—*John Glenn*

A birthday is just the first day of another 365-day journey around the sun. Enjoy the trip.
—*Author Unknown*

Youth is a wonderful thing. What a crime to waste it on children.
—*George Bernard Shaw*

MOTHER AND CHILD

A mother holds a child's hand for an instant but their heart forever.
—*Author Unknown*

Babies are such a nice way to start people.
—*Don Herold*

A baby is God's opinion that the world should go on.
—*Carl Sandburg*

The lives of a Mother and Daughter are forever sweetly intertwined.
—*Author Unknown*

Flowers have the sun, children have their mothers.
—*Author Unknown*

You never get over being a child, as long as you have a mother to go to.
—*Sarah Jewett*

A mother understands what a child does not say.
—*Jewish Proverb*

Never have children, only grandchildren
—*Gore Vidal*

SYMPATHY AND SUPPORT

Courage is fear that has said its prayers.
—*Dorothy Bernard*

Memories keep those we love close forever.
—*Author Unknown*

The world is full of suffering. It is also full of the overcoming of it.
—*Helen Keller*

We cannot direct the wind, but we can adjust our sails.
—*Bertha Calloway*

Thank goodness for rainy days!
Without them, we wouldn't have rainbows.
—*Author Unknown*

Perhaps they are not stars in the sky but rather openings in the heaven, where the love of our lost ones pours through and shines down to let us know they are happy.
—*Eskimo Proverb*

To climb steep hills requires a slow pace at first.
—*William Shakespeare*

LOVE

Love does not consist in gazing at each other but in looking outward together in the same direction.
—*Antoine de Saint-Exupéry*

The best and most beautiful things cannot be seen or even touched, they must be felt with the heart.
—*Helen Keller*

Here's hoping that you live forever
And mine is the last voice you hear.
—*Willard Scott*

Love is the master key that unlocks the gates of happiness.
—*Oliver Wendell Holmes*

You don't marry one person, you marry three: the person you think they are, the person they are, and the person they are going to become as the result of being married to you.
—*Richard Needham*

In your hands my heart found a home.
—*Author Unknown*

I fall in love with you over and over again.
—*Author Unknown*

There is only one happiness in life, to love and be loved.

—*George Sand*

FRIENDSHIP

The better part of one's life consists of his friendships.

—*Abraham Lincoln*

Every man who is high up loves to think that he has done it all himself; and the wife smiles and lets it go at that.

—*James Matthew Barrie*

Today, something happened—the simplest of things really—but I found myself wishing you were here to share it with me.

—*Harris*

There are good ships, and there are wood ships, the ships that sail the sea. But the best ships are friendships, and may they always be.

—*an Irish Blessing*

A good friend is someone who thinks you're a good egg, even though you're slightly cracked.

—*Bernard Meltzer*

May your troubles be less and your blessings be more, and nothing but happiness come through your door.

—*An Irish Blessing*

May you see only rainbows, feel only happiness, hear only music.

—*Author Unknown*

The only way to have a friend is to be one.

—*Ralph Waldo Emerson*

A friend is someone who
understands your past,
believes in your future
and loves you today,
just the way you are.

—*Author Unknown*

Side by side, or miles apart,
Dear friends are always close at heart.

—*Author Unknown*

We have a strange and wonderful relationship.
You're strange
And I'm wonderful!

—*Author Unknown*

A friend gathers your scattered pieces and gives them back to you in the right order.
A friend is a crutch when you've sprained your big toe.
A friend is the mulch that makes conversations grow.
But most of all a friend is there . . .
. . . when you've tucked your shirt in your underwear!

—*Author Unknown*

We've been through a lot together . . .
. . . and most of it was your fault.
—*Author Unknown*

Write it on your heart that every day is the best day of the year.
—*Ralph Waldo Emerson*

Your wealth is where your friends are.
—*Plato*

HOLIDAYS

May your holidays be wonderful, and wonder-full.

Blessed are those who see Christmas through the eyes of a child.

Easter is the only time that it's perfectly safe to put all your eggs in one basket.

Colorful candles burning bright, each lit on eight very special nights.

May the lights of Hanukkah usher in a better world for all humankind.

—*Jewish Proverb*

OTHER SENTIMENTS

You Inspire Me.
—*Author Unknown*

Hitch your wagon to a star.
—*Ralph Waldo Emerson*

Children are poor man's riches.
—*English Proverb*

A good laugh is sunshine in a house.
—*William Makepeace Thackeray*

A house is built with walls and beams,
But a home is built of Love and Dreams.
—*Author Unknown*

He who laughs last didn't get it.
—*Author Unknown*

I ask not for a lighter burden, but for broader shoulders.
—*Jewish Proverb*

Sometimes those who have given us the most are the ones we fail to thank. I thank you now.
—*Author Unknown*

Resources

3M Worlswide

www.3m.com

Glue, glue sticks, and foam adhesive

7 gypsies

www.sevengypsies.com

Scrapbook paper, embellishments, journals, albums, and paper craft supplies

Anna Griffin

www.annagriffin.com

Scrapbook paper, albums, embellishments, and stationery supplies

Art Institute Glitter, Inc.

www.artglitter.com

Glitter, glitter adhesive, and glitter tools

Artistic Wire Ltd.

www.artisticwire.com

Wire and wire working tools

Creative Imaginations

www.creativeimaginations.us

Scrapbook paper, embellishments, and paper craft supplies

Die Cuts With A View

www.diecutswithaview.com

Cardstock and decorative paper and paper pads, albums, and embellishments

Heidi Swapp

www.heidiswapp.com

Decorative paper, albums, decorative tape, and embellishments

Inkadinkado

www.inkadinkado.com

Stamps, inks, stencils, and rubber stamping accessories

Jacquard Products

www.jacquardproducts.com

Fabric paint and dyes, inks, acrylic paints, powdered pigments, and metallic stamp pads

K&Company

www.kandcompany.com

Scrapbook paper, albums, embellishments, and rub-ons

Making Memories

www.makingmemories.com

Scrapbook paper, albums, eyelets and eyelet setting tools, stickers, rub-ons, and embellishments

Martha Stewart Crafts

www.marthastewartcrafts.com

Embellishments, tools, paper, stationery, storage, organization, wrapping and food packaging, scrapbooking supplies, entertaining supplies, and kids crafts

Paper Source

www.paper-source.com

Paper, stickers, rubber stamps, embellishments, envelopes and cards, and book binding supplies, including waxed twine

Plaid/All Night Media

www.plaidonline.com

Rubber stamps, decorative paper, paints, decoupage adhesive, inks, punches, markers, and rub-ons

Postmodern Design
P.O. Box 720416
Norman, OK 73072
405-321-3176
405-321-2296 (fax)
Rubber stamps

Prism
www.prismpapers.com
Scrapbook paper

Ranger Industries
www.rangerink.com
*Rubber stamps, pigment, dye, alcohol, and
Distress inks, embossing ink and powders*

Sakura
www.gellyroll.com
Soufflé, Glaze, and Micron pens, markers

SEI
www.shopsei.com
Scrapbook paper, albums, embellishments, and dyes

Stampendous
www.stampendous.com
*Rubber stamps, embossing powder, glitter, tags,
stickers, and cards and envelopes, including vellum
envelopes*

Stampington & Company
www.stampington.com
Rubber stamps, magazines, and paper art supplies

Tsukineko
www.tsukineko.com
*Pigment, dye, and craft inks, markers, embossing
powders, and sponge daubers*

We R Memory Keepers
www.weronthenet.com
*Decorative paper, scrapbook albums, chipboard
embellishments, eyelets and eyelet setting tools,
rub-ons, metal embellishments*

Xyron
www.xyron.com
*Wishblade die cutter, Design Runner personal
printer, and adhesives*

Acknowledgments

For watching my girls,
thanks to my friends—
I know my work seems like
It never quite ends.

For being utterly patient,
I must thank my girls.
And thanks to my husband
For helping balance my worlds.

Mary Ann, Regina, Pat,
And Kevin from Quarry—
Thank you for helping me
Write this card story.

And finally thanks to
All those who make art.
You inspire my work
And feed my heart.

About the Author

Jenn Mason lives, works, creates, and teaches by the motto, "She is able who thinks she's able." When she's not writing a book, composing a magazine column, designing product, teaching workshops, or hosting a webisode for CraftTVWeekly.com, she is either happily telling stories through paint, collage, and assemblage in her Brookline, Massachusetts, studio or spending quality time with her husband and two young girls in their 150-year-old carriage house. She is the author of several books, including the most recent: *The Art of the Family Tree* (Quarry Books, 2007). Jenn can be reached through her website at www.jennmason.com.